Salisbury, England
Magnum photojournalist Ian Berry

Ian Berry...
«The Quiet Man of Magnum»

John Cogan

Front cover:
Xiahe, Gansu Province, China
Novice Tibetan monks on their way to prayer
Back cover:
Ian Berry - photograph by John Cogan

ISBN 978-1-3999-9085-1

Allies-Group Ltd
Enterprise House
Kingsway
Team Valley Trading Estate
Gateshead
NE11 0SR

allies-group.com

ALLIESGROUP

This book is a product of the collective inputs of many selfless voices. There are many to acknowledge. However, those I wish to name are the following:

1. The late Jurgen Schadeburg for his time spent taking me back to the late 1950s and early 1960s

2. Amanda Hopkinson, the daughter of the late Sir Tom Hopkinson, for her enthusiastic support and allowing me to quote from her father's writings.

3. Ruth Hoffmann of Magnum Photos for her encouragement and support.

4. My fellow photographers and good friends Dr John Clarke and Tony Griffiths for their advice, encouragement and corrections.

5. My son, Ross, for encouraging me and keeping me on my toes, and for his wonderful grasp of English, which is no surprise given that he's a poet.

6. Chris March, Euan Underwood and the staff at Allies Group for their hard work and commitment to the book.

And then there is Ian himself without whom the book would have been nothing more than blank pages.

This book is dedicated to our wives, Kathie and Angela, for their patience, support and enwcouragement.

With thanks to Eliza Williams, Creative Review, 09/05/2007

John Cogan, 2024

Contents

Just a brief word before we get started

When you start to read this book and look at the photographs contained within, please remember that, as far as Ian Berry is concerned, this is a work in progress. It is not a summation or even a retrospective in the true sense of the word. There is an implication of something final in both those words. As far as Ian Berry is concerned, this is most certainly **not** the case.

This book sets out to provide the reader with an understanding of the work of one of Britain's most able and talented photographers, one whose breadth of work and achievements can so easily be overlooked because of the modesty of the man. There is an allied factor in that most of Ian's work over the years has been aimed at magazines and newspapers, and being a hardworking photographer, once a story was filed he moved onto the next.

Many of his contemporaries have become known for either a particular genre of photography or for producing books that are very specific and revelatory. As for Ian's work, the fact that he covers a wide range of subjects means you will find it difficult to allocate a genre to him. The other difficulty here is that Ian Berry dislikes labels and categories. He is not a war photographer but has photographed war. He is not a specialist portrait photographer but has photographed some of the most influential people of their day ranging from actors to film stars to politicians, writers and musicians.

Ian is not a specialist travel photographer though he has travelled to many countries and his work has graced some of the most influential of travel magazines such as *Condé Nast Traveller* and the Hamburg-based magazine *Geo*.

Could we say that Ian is a photojournalist? Well, he's a journalist and a photographer who has photographed just about everything, especially when working on stories for newspapers and magazines.

Ian Berry FRPS is now the longest-serving, full member of *Magnum Photos*. As we follow his career in the next few pages, we will be able to make up our own mind as to the power of his photographs, especially when we see his work. That is the real purpose of this book: to provide the reader with as comprehensive a view as possible of Ian Berry's achievements and, at the same time, see how one man has chronicled the times we live in.

Ian has borne witness to over 60 years of history since his pictures were first published back in the late 1950s. to the present day he has born witness to over 60 years of history. Very few other photographers can claim that. But this is an on-going story for Ian is still out there with his camera, taking his pictures unobserved. In such diverse venues as his home town of Salisbury, and outside the Palace of Westminster, Ian Berry continues to record events, forever looking for a story.

It is for the reader to give thoughtful consideration to the work of Ian Berry and experience the human condition though his images. Those images will speak for themselves. My words are mere noises off.

A final word from the author. There are three discrete voices in this narrative. There is obviously Ian Berry's voice in both words and pictures. There are the voices of those who worked alongside him and, finally, there is that of the author. The convention is that Ian Berry is given his full name at the beginning and thereafter known as Berry. Over the years since we first met I hope we have become friends and he is known to me as Ian, as I am know as John to him. To resort to something that sounds impersonal is to run counter to how we behave towards each other. I only hope this is acceptable to all our readers.

Ian Berry

"You have to remember that, at the end of the day, you're just a photographer — not a brain surgeon."

Ian Berry

Ian Berry sits opposite me, across the small circular table in the Oak Bar, The Rose and Crown in Salisbury has become our regular meeting place when we need to talk over the material for his biography.

On this occasion, we are discussing a trip he made to the venue of one of his stories. As the story begins to unfold, Ian's description seems sparse, but his words are only a preamble to the images, those visual realities which offer us all the chance to see beyond the "official".

In all his work (and during our time together), Ian is nothing if not discreet and perceptive. Whilst some photographers try to stand on their dignity, demanding this and that, becoming more the story than the story itself, Ian prefers not to be brash and make demands. In many of the places where he has ventured, his gentle, measured yet firm approach has opened more doors for him than would otherwise be the case.

Whilst Ian talks, I make my notes. There is something mesmeric in the way he unfolds a story: quiet and thoughtful. Ian exudes a Zen-like calm. Beyond the coffee cups, he sits, one leg crossed over the other. They remain crossed throughout the next hour or so. He moves very little and every move is deliberate. Though he "seems" physically hunched, it is a delusion, for he has this habit, seemingly, of withdrawing into himself. This is a smokescreen. Ian is always ready. Years of "being ready" becomes more than a habit. It is ingrained. His face shows little by way of emotion. Years of disappearing into the background, becoming the wallpaper, suits his chameleon-like persona.

Selecting a cube of sugar from the mini Kilner jar, Ian holds it in the coffee and slowly feeds it through the meniscus and into the liquid. The coffee absorbs the cube, and the sugar cube takes up the coffee. This could be a metaphor for Ian's approach to the way he works. When I look at his face it is obvious that he is constantly thinking, processing the scene, doing what a photojournalist would be doing: assessing.

Later, we walk to Salisbury Cathedral to enjoy the delights of their refectory. Ian misses little. He has a compact way of walking that is neither too fast nor too slow, but very measured. Whilst in the Cathedral's cloister something attracts his attention and his camera is out and used before you are aware of what he is doing.

We enter the nave. Standing a little to one side we can observe the reactions of the many visitors to a work of art that is secular in construction. It is large, about eight feet high by six feet wide and is spectacularly colourful. Sadly, it is universally ignored by most of the people who enter the nave. When someone does pay it attention, Ian takes careful note. There is something ambiguous about the artwork and it is the reaction of the visitors to this installation that fascinates him.

Ian Berry was born in Preston, Lancashire. He attended two private schools, but we don't talk much about his past life. There is a very British reserve in the way Ian considers these aspects of his story. He would rather not burden his audience with any details he regards as irrelevant. A lifetime of blending into the background is a hard carapace to shed.

What you do glean are the crumbs he lets slip: his father used to drive racing cars and he was given a very good camera early in his life, a Zeiss. This camera led him to experiment with lighting which, as it so happened, caused him to burn the back of the family's leather sofa.

Ian joined Magnum Photos in 1962. He is an Honorary Fellow of the Royal Photographic Society, was the first contract photographer employed by the Observer magazine and the first photographer to be awarded an Arts Council of Great Britain grant which resulted in his landmark book, *The English.*

Early in his career, he worked in South Africa and famously recorded the shootings at Sharpeville in 1960.

Visiting and re-visiting South Africa over the years, Ian has continued to record both the struggle of the people to rid themselves of apartheid and the subsequent birth of the Rainbow Nation in all its complexity. From his vast experience he produced the definitive book, *Living Apart*. An observer of wider African changes, he photographed the birth pangs of the Congo, in 1960-61. He has been shot at and arrested as a spy (several times) and spent time in the horrific conditions of an African prison. And still he continues his quest for a story.

Nearer to home he has shared discussions about roses with the then German Chancellor Konrad Adenauer, sat in a pub with the Irish poet Seamus Heaney and flirted with the opera singer Kiri Te Kanawa over a game of golf. Recently, he has spent time with then Labour leader Jeremy Corbyn, whilst Corbyn was canvassing during a General Election. When you consider the range of assignments Ian has completed my biggest fear in embarking upon this biography is that there will not be enough space in these pages to cover such a life lived less ordinary.

Nottingham, England

Ian Berry at a Royal Photographic Society workshop, thanks to Stewart Wall of the Royal Photographic Society

Back in the day

"The great single picture is emotionally satisfying, whereas getting a good journalistic story is more about being a professional."

Ian Berry

In Castleford Public Library's non-fiction collection were copies of the now-defunct *Photography Year Book*. This was an annual review of photography published by the *Photography* magazine. The year book for 1962 contained a selection of Star Photographers, along with a brief essay written by the then editor, the Australian Norman Hall. One of the stars featured in the 1962 edition was Ian Berry. Hall had selected four photographs to illustrate his article. In praising Ian as being the most reliable of photographers Hall went on to say "*Whenever there is trouble he is present, restless and relentless in his anxiety to present a faithful record of the event". Hall continued "But not just trouble – though the times produce more than a fair share of this: Ian is an all-round photographer who can turn in a portfolio of superb ballet pictures, a straight portrait or a series of thrilling shots from a sporting sequence. He is one of the world's best photo-journalists and I take pleasure in saluting him here."*

Those four images were monochrome images photographed in South Africa when Ian was working for *Drum*, the African magazine. Each one concentrated upon a person (or people) as they responded to the situations in which they found themselves. One was a full-page portrait of an African miner waiting to join the rescue squad at the notorious *Coalbrook* mine disaster. The disaster occurred on 21st January 1960 when 433 men were killed.

The second photograph was of an African patient suffering from pneumonia. He was being transported to hospital on a bullock-drawn sledge. The hospital was run by Dr Anthony Barker and his wife. They left South Africa a little later, only to both die in a cycling accident in the English Lake District. Of this photograph, Ian's memory is clear. He was visiting the clinic to watch an operation. The Barkers suggested he should have a cup of coffee beforehand. Ian chose not to. That was a big mistake. Offering some sympathy later as Ian looked nauseous, he was told he should have had his coffee first, **then** observe the operation.

The most memorable image for me is a photograph taken in 1960 in Maseru, Basutoland (now Lesotho). It shows a group of men standing outside a large, official-looking building in the midst of a dust storm. They wait for the results of a ballot to elect their new Paramount Chief. If ever there was a single image that encapsulates the power a single photograph has to tell a story it is this one. Even without knowing the story, the viewer cannot but be impressed by the stoicism of the men waiting, nor can you fail to "feel" the power of the wind and the sting of the driven dust.

The last of those pictures chosen by Hall is the portrait of a young schoolboy. It was part of a story Ian was covering: one about malnutrition amongst school children. The boy is framed by a window as he sits there listening to the teacher. There is a more powerful light coming through the opposite window so the boy is very much back lit.

Through the various *Photography Year Books* I became aware of the power a single image can have and followed the work of those photographers who became my eyes to a world far removed from the Yorkshire coalfield where I grew up.

Maseru, Basutoland (Lesotho)
Basutos caught in a dust storm outside the legislative building shield themselves with the thick blankets they wear

Meeting Ian Berry for the first time

Whilst writing for the Royal Photographic Society about the work of various documentary photographers, I had a chance to meet Ian over a meal at the *Brasserie Blanc* in Covent Garden. It was at this meeting that the idea for a book about his life was first mentioned. Over the next few years we met to discuss various aspects of Ian's working life. There was no doubt in both our minds that here were stories and photographs that had the makings of a book. The only problem was that I would become excited by a story and its associated photographs, and Ian would say *"Do you really think anyone would be interested in that. The pictures were not that good."*

Ian Berry is a very modest gentleman. He is also very affable. What he is not is someone who will divulge anything that may embarrass anyone else. Thankfully, I am not interested in risqué stories and Ian is not interested in telling me any. So, there are no exposes of dark or devious doings in the following pages. There are, however, times when the narrative will read more like a *Boy's Own* paper, and others when you have to wonder if there isn't one of the gods of comedy exerting some influence.

Why hadn't Ian written such a book before? *"Some years I was so busy I just went from one job to another without a pause for breath. It's what I did."* Ian Berry's reputation rests upon his body of work. One recent gallery owner, when Ian's name was mentioned, immediately responded with enthusiasm. *"He's a wonderful photographer. His work is great."*

It is also fair to say that he is known as *"The Quiet Man of Magnum", and the "Photographers' Photographer."*

As for his membership of Magnum: *"There were those of us who brought in the money. Back then it would be Burt (Glinn), Rene (Burri), Marc Riboud and Abbas along with others. You could say it was our commercial assignments that kept Magnum afloat."*

After we managed to secure a publisher, Ian's first concern was whether the print quality would do justice to his photographs. My concern was whether being Ian's Boswell, could I do justice to my Dr Johnson? Granted, Ian is far from being a roly- poly, periwigged gentleman and I'm no nimble Scot but the thought is there. One thing I discovered early on was that the severest critic of Ian Berry's work is Ian Berry himself. When we talked about the Sharpeville shootings *"They're not really good photographs. It was all too rushed. The fact that I had been in the line of fire, shot at even, though not hit, meant that my fellow journalists inflated my importance. Why they seem to think that is something of a badge of honour I have no idea. I've been in worse situations than that."* If he had to choose from that sequence it *might* result in the selection of a single image.

Every photograph you will see has been chosen by Ian. To arrive at the final images he will have applied some complex set of variables, to do with shape and context and lighting. From my point of view, I look at a different set of criteria. I'm interested in the illustrating capacity which might be something as simple as an insight into a news item or a capacity to tell a story.

Salisbury, England
Ian Berry

Africa

"Few people have captured the mood of Africa in quite the same way as photographer Ian Berry."

Norman Hall, Photography Year Book for 1963

Several Commonwealth nations were in need of immigrants after the losses they suffered during the Second World War: Australia, Canada, New Zealand and South Africa were all willing people to come. Those were the days of the £10 Pom.

Ian decided upon South Africa, because his parents had links with a South African photographer. Roger Madden was willing to sponsor Ian, who also fancied the chance to see the wild life. Arriving in South Africa as a sixteen year old, Ian Berry went to work for Madden. Roger Madden had been assistant to Ansel Adams, the renowned American landscape photographer, and was able to give the young Ian Berry a good grounding in classic photographic techniques. Madden was a commercial photographer and this invariably meant the use of a large format, plate camera. Because of their bulk and weight, these cameras needed a very substantial tripod to keep them steady. They were slow to use, and produced a single, large negative.

Working in the digital age, when the results are instantaneous, many mistakes can be corrected later either in camera or on a computer. Not so with the large format *Linhof.* Whatever their limitations, these cameras did teach the beginner to adopt careful and considered approach. The framing of the image and care taken with the composition are essentials when using such cameras, as all necessary adjustments must be made prior to pressing the shutter. The slowness of the process and the single negative mean that there are few chances to revisit a photograph. However, such care pays dividends when the resultant negative is crisp, clear and provides you with a potential positive image of considerable size.

After leaving Madden, Ian set out to run his own photographic business. It was whilst travelling from village to village that he met a fellow immigrant: the Berlin-born Jürgen Schadeberg. Working with Schadeberg, Ian spent his free time photographing weddings. It soon became clear that weddings were not *"my cup of tea".* The thought of spending his life producing formal, static portraits, all the while keeping the mother of the bride happy, did not appeal. It would invariably mean compromising his own developing photographic aesthetic. Journalism in some form or another beckoned, and using a camera rather than a pen was what most attracted him. Once again, Schadeberg helped by introducing Ian to several newspaper editors.

At various times Ian worked for the *Rand Daily Mail* and the South African *Sunday Times*. There were periods when Ian was the chief photographer on short-lived African papers *EGoli* and the *Benoni City Times*. It was whilst working for the *Rand Daily Mail*, that Ian was assigned to cover the infamous 1956 Treason Trials. The South African Government had passed a Suppression of Communism Act that became the means of arresting 156 people they regarded as a threat to the continued application of apartheid. Amongst the 156 arrested and put on trial was Nelson Mandela. Mandela's book *Long Walk to Freedom* features many of Ian's photographs.

When it became known that Tom Hopkinson was coming to take over as editor of *Drum* magazine, Ian saw an opportunity to further develop his skills as a magazine photographer. Drum was the magazine in which to have your photographs of African life published. Tom Hopkinson, later to become Sir Tom Hopkinson, was already established in Britain as an editor par excellence. His editorship of Picture Post had been instrumental in making it a worthy rival to America's Life Magazine. However, when Bert Hardy's photographs and James Cameron's article about the treatment of the North Korean prisoners during the Korean War were withdrawn by the magazine's owners he resigned. Now he was coming to South Africa.

Drum was the African magazine produced by Africans, for an African readership. As an African magazine it had already exposed several major scandals, and was a publication to which Ian had submitted photographs as a freelance. These had been well received and it helped that the picture editor was his old friend, Jürgen Schadeberg. When Tom Hopkinson saw Ian's photographs he was happy to offer him a permanent post.

The camera Ian had been forced to use when working on the newspapers was the traditional press camera: the Speed Graphic. It was yet another heavyweight camera, unwieldy and slow, but it produced an image of a size and clarity beloved by newspaper picture editors. Following a shift in fashion and utility, the Speed Graphic gave way to the more flexible and lighter Rolleiflex. This camera still produced a negative of sufficient size to warm the cockles of a picture editor's heart. It was a roll film camera, rather than the clumsy single sheets of the Graphic, and this invariably meant more frames being available when on assignment. It was also faster and less obtrusive for the photographer to use.

Harrismith, Orange Free State, South Africa
A rather nervous nanny with her white charge at a National Party meeting where she is the only black person

Transvaal (Gauteng), South Africa
Coffin bearers give the ANC clenched fist salute at the funeral of a schoolgirl shot by the police at an earlier funeral

As the 1950s slowly edged towards the 1960s the Rollei became ubiquitous in the hands of photojournalists and newspaper photographers. However, the Rolleiflex (for all its good qualities) was giving way to what was to become the default camera of the photojournalist, the 35mm Leica. This was smaller than even the Rollei, was easier to carry and could be used with a choice of various sizes of lens. Best of all, it was very quiet.

As we have seen, Ian Berry is variously described as unobtrusive and able to blend in, like wallpaper. With a Leica in his hand, Ian had found the ideal camera to match his style of working. Sometimes wearing a jacket that was slightly too big (where he could hide the camera), Ian would also adopt Henri Cartier-Bresson's advice to walk slowly (thereby avoiding attracting attention). Suitably accoutred Ian was now free to prowl whenever and wherever there was anything to photograph. He became that silent, ghost-like figure who would spend the rest of his life being inconspicuous, moving stealthily and becoming at one with the background.

Apart from being with Tom Hopkinson, Ian found other advantages to working at *Drum*. He was able to spend a lot of time with the African photographers and journalists employed in Drum. At the end of the day, as the office was emptying, Ian could discuss photography with one of the young African photographers, a youth eager to learn from Ian. This was Ernest Cole, who was to become a noted "voice" in what has become known in South Africa as Liberation Photography. The other African photographer who worked alongside Ian was Peter Magubane, another Liberation Photographer who became *Time Life's* man in South Africa.

Fordsburg, Johannesburg, South Africa
A tender moment in an all-black café where music is performed, encouraging liberal whites to attend. Many of the musicians such as Hugh Masakele went on to become famous world wide

Stellenbosch, South Africa

An auction of fine wines at the Nederburg estate in the Cape Province where coloured workers bring further supplies to the wine tasting

Zululand, South Africa
An elderly man with pneumonia living far from any town is being taken to hospital by 'field ambulance'

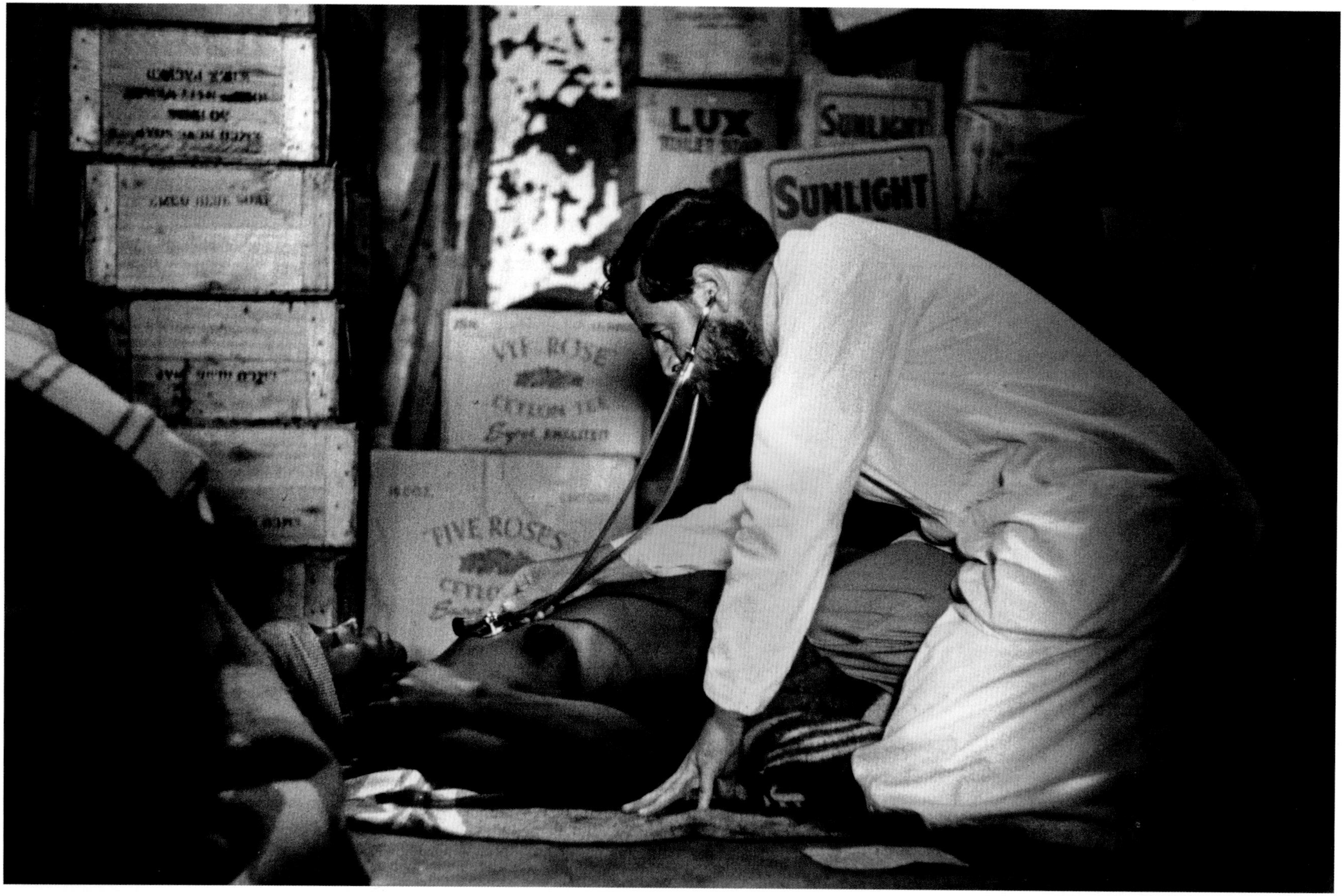

Zululand, South Africa

Where there are no clinics, Anthony Barker, a mission doctor, treats patients on the floor of a trading store warehouse

Daily life at Drum

"Tom Hopkinson, ex-editor of Picture Post, *became the editor [of* Drum*] and I wanted to learn about magazine photography from a man whose reputation had preceded him... One difficulty we did not have on* Drum *was jealousy over assignments between the black and white members. The only question asked was who could do a given job best".*

Ian Berry

Ian is very clear that, during his eighteen months at *Drum*, the two events of greatest significance to him were, firstly, the shootings at Sharpeville (with all its ramifications), and the second was working with Tom Hopkinson. It was during Hopkinson's tenure that Ian learned the skill of producing photographs that would see his work being consistently published in magazines.

The bread-and-butter assignments that filled the pages of *Drum* could be about anything, and usually were. Yet, apart from the single issue assignments that meant a couple of photographs to illustrate an article, Ian learned to produce a photographic essay for a major article. These were usually about something of significance to the lives of many Africans.

One assignment took him onto the streets of Johannesburg to photograph the musician Spoke Mashiyane who would entertain the crowds with his penny whistle. Yet, another month would see Ian travel to Cape Town to produce an in-depth story about the notorious District Six (aka The Seven Steps). Though all these assignments might seem run-of-the-mill now, it should be remembered that this was a time when the Nationalist Party took every opportunity to strengthen its hold over the lives and futures of the African population. The true ramifications of their apartheid policy were becoming clear. Nothing was ever apolitical, and when Ian went to photograph the Kutlwanong home for African deaf, dumb and blind children he brought back a sequence of fine portraits of children and their teachers which elsewhere would be seen as a moving story but in South Africa had a political subtext, with provision for children of colour being at the heart of the article.

The Nationalist Government believed something as basic as educating disabled children needed to conform to their policy of separate development. Looking at those pictures now, distanced from the social and political context in which they were made, Ian's compassion is very evident in the way he portrayed the children and the staff.

Tom Hopkinson brought with him a European sensibility and demanded rigour from his staff. His first impressions of the *Drum* offices were less than favourable: *"The gaunt building which housed the* Drum *offices stood at the extreme edge of this central part of the city, in a district where the skyscrapers dwindled down into a shambles of small factories, arid waste patches... half built-over lots of second-hand car dealers..."* Tom Hopkinson

Northern Transvaal (Gauteng), South Africa
A white couple leave their child in the care of a black nanny, little more than a child herself

Inside the building, *"The Drum offices, on the first floor, consisted of about a dozen glass-partitioned rooms. Blue-painted pillars carried a low whitewashed ceiling. The linoleum on the floor was new, but so thin... Ours was not much of a place, but in one respect it was, in that city, almost unique, for within these walls, there was no apartheid - no separate entrances for blacks and no separate lifts (this was easy because there was no lift at all). Blacks and whites sat side by side, made use of the same washbasins and lavatories and drank out of the same teacups..."* Tom Hopkinson

Hopkinson's intentions was to make the magazine a more prestigious publication, but this would require it to look better than a "Dime Novel". To that end it needed to be printed on better quality paper. When he presented his intentions to Jim Bailey, Hopkinson's suggestion was met with disdain. As far as Bailey was concerned, producing a better quality magazine meant higher costs, especially when the South African government deliberately restricted Drum's access to paper. What Bailey bought was poor quality newsprint, because it was cheap and ruffled no feathers. It would be a further irony that, should they use better paper, printing with a different (and more expensive printer) would be necessary. There was only one available at that time and Hopkinson would need to send his copy to presses owned by the Verwoerd family. This family was a cornerstone of the Afrikaner community, one of whom was Hendrik, prime minister of the Union Of South Africa from 1958 until 1961, when he became the prime minister of the Republic of South Africa until his assassination in 1966.

Working at *Drum* meant constant harassment by the South African Police (SAP). On many an occasion Tom Hopkinson would regularly attend police stations to "retrieve" one or more of his staff.

"I'd accompany Tom to the local prison to bail out Drum staff who'd been locked up for being in a certain area, or because their pass wasn't quite in order, or some 17-year-old policeman from the platteland had taken a dislike to them for being a cheeky kaffir." Ian Berry

The photographer, Peter Magubane, was often singled out for aggressive attention; usually accused of stealing the camera(s) he always carried.

"Peter was a sturdy, thick-set figure with an open face and determination in every line. He had the habit of wrinkling up his brow when talking, as if speech were a matter demanding concentration. At 26-27 he was one of the oldest members of our staff, having made his way up by way of being, first a driver, then a dark-room assistant; he was fond of good clothes and always drove a big American convertible." Tom Hopkinson

When it came to harassment by the police, official SAP figures for the reporting year 1958-59 speak for themselves. They show that 1,250,000 Africans were jailed for Pass Law infringements, abuse of liquor regulations, movement control and curfew violations. With such pressure from the authorities, and the harrowing conditions of township life, it was little wonder alcohol abuse was rife.

One SAP harassment went too far, and this involved *Drum's* office boy, Sidney Andrews. Sidney was a slightly built and educated young African. Any *Drum* worker was fair game, especially an educated one. Besides, to the Afrikaner, anyone who worked on *Drum* must be a communist. Sidney was frequently arrested. On this particular evening the beating got out of hand and Sidney was taken to the casualty ward for Non-Europeans at the General Hospital. Talking to the duty doctor, Hopkinson asked her to make sure she kept a record of his injuries. *"I always keep careful notes of these police assault cases,"* she replied.

Leaving the hospital, Hopkinson sent a message to Ian, asking him to get round to the hospital and photograph Sidney's wounds. At 1am. as Hopkinson was about to retire for the night, he noticed a slip of paper on the hall floor: *"Picture taken. Ian"*

Later Sidney was charged with assaulting a police officer. In the subsequent court case Ian's photographs were used to support the claim that the young, fragile-looking Sidney had been unlikely to have assaulted the large, powerful and martial-arts trained police officer. The case was dismissed. There was a corollary to the story. One of the journalists at the *Golden City Post* saw Ian's prints and sent one of them, the most horrific of the sequence, to a London daily newspaper who printed it with the headlines **"The face that should shock the world"**

It was Bailey's interference with the editorial work of Tom Hopkinson's immediate predecessor, Sylvester Stein, that drove Stein to resign. The last straw as far as Stein was concerned was over his choice of a photograph for one of *Drum's* covers. Stein had chosen an image of the African-American tennis player Althea Gibson, the first woman of colour to win Wimbledon. Pictures of the event had been widely circulated around the world. This had made Gibson a star. Stein's choice was one of the most spectacular photographs which showed a jubilant Gibson kissing her white opponent on the cheek. Stein had the cover ready to be printed and left Can Themba, his editorial assistant, in charge. Stein was leaving on a pre-planned field trip.

When making the choice, Stein believed that Bailey would baulk at publishing this image, especially on the cover. In the hope of preventing Bailey's interference he had kept quiet and made sure everything was ready for the printing. Believing the layout and printing processes were too far advanced to be changed, Stein felt confident that Themba could handle the rest of the publication. With faith in his assistant's abilities, Stein left for his trip.

However, his initial instincts had been correct. No sooner had he left for his trip than Bailey forced Themba to pull the Althea Gibson photograph. Bailey's interference with his editor's autonomy was a recurring theme throughout not only Stein's tenure but Hopkinson's as well.

"When you first met him (Jim Bailey) it was all 'hail fellow, well met!' Over time the reality of the man became clear. It's safe to say he wasn't one of the good guys." Ian Berry

The *Drum* photographic archive is considerable. After Bailey's death, when Peter Magubane sought the return of his negatives, they were discovered in old filing cabinets in a barn on Bailey's farm. Those images now form a vital part of the official South African Archive. Searching online they offer a chance to view the illustrated history of those troubled times.

As a further example of interference, Tom Hopkinson had planned a feature for the April 1960 edition. This was to be about the *Pan African Congress* (PAC). The bulk of African resistance to apartheid came from the African National Congress (ANC), but there were those in the townships who believed more radical action should be adopted. They had formed the PAC as a breakaway group. Hopkinson wanted to explore the differences and highlight the work of the PAC. Bailey would have none of it! He feared any article that the government believed to be dangerous, or inflammatory, would bring about the closure of the magazine.

Bailey took the same stance over Ian's photographs of the Sharpeville shootings and Humphrey Tyler's written account. It would be a good six months before the Sharpeville pictures and the account appeared in South Africa.

To meet what he saw as his target audience, Bailey wanted girls, girls and even more girls. He felt the magazine cover was only successful if it featured a girl, the more scantily clad the better. One of the favourite models was the singer and actress Dolly Rathebe. Neither Ian nor Peter were allowed to take the cover picture. That was Jürgen Schadeberg's prerogative. In a way, cover girls made sense as the majority of the readership was male and illiterate. Young men coming to work in the mines needing a distraction. That belief lay at the heart of Bailey's intentions behind the format and purpose of *Drum*.

Asking Ian about being white amongst black journalists, was there the potential that covering a story must have been easier for him than Peter Magubane? Surely, his colour protected him from the SAP?

"Not really." To the Afrikaners, being one of the hated English was bad enough. The fact that Ian was quietly spoken, self-effacing and polite, had a ready, affable smile and did little to draw attention to himself only made matters worse. You would think that the SAP would find little in Ian's demeanour to offend them. Yet those very features proclaimed Ian as a Brit and that was the equivalent to a red rag waved in a bull's face!

Granted, in one way, this look served him well. It proved to the Africans he met that he was sympathetic and helped him on many an occasion when he was photographing aspects of African life.

"I never had any trouble from the Africans. It was always the Afrikaner who were the problem. They hated the English almost as much as they hated the Africans. The police threatened to kill me several times, and they meant it." Ian Berry.

Needing little provocation and seeing him with his camera, the SAP regularly took pleasure in threatening Ian. Working on a particular story about SAP action in a township, Ian followed a white SAP officer as he chased two African youths along a township street. The youths turned a corner and disappeared. Frustrated by being cheated of his prize, the Afrikaner officer focused all his anger on Ian. Lashing out with his *sjambok*, the officer smashed into Ian's chest breaking a virtually indestructible Leica camera lens and cracking several of Ian's ribs.

It was whilst Ian was recuperating from the attack that it was someone's bright idea to photograph "The Best Place in South Africa to have a Holiday". Whether this was meant as a joke or a serious attempt at satire Ian never knew. Instead, he ended up in the town of Luderitz, in South West Africa (now Namibia). The 21st century has since seen it develop into a fashionable holiday destination but when Ian arrived it was anything but.

Hatred of the English by the Afrikaners lasted a long time. Later in his career, Ian returned to South Africa and was fortunate to accompany an Estonian colleague on a visit to the ultra-nationalist Eugène Terre'Blanche. The only way Ian could "survive" this visit intact was to remain silent and let everyone believe him to be Estonian.

In choosing Ian, Tom Hopkinson recognised his innate skill when it came to producing a sequence of photographs that would tell a ready-made, coherent story. Hopkinson had worked with some of the great European photojournalists and knew how effective their stories could be. Whilst writers like Can Themba could produce racy stories in an American, pulp fiction style, one that certainly suited the magazine's readership, Hopkinson also realised the written text catered for less than half of *Drum's* audience. Images *spoke* to the illiterate half of *Drum's* customers. These were the transient mine workers and township youth who, apart from scantily clad women, wanted photographs of musicians, singers and sportsmen.

Drum regularly featured township music. These stories were usually written by the African musicians employed by *Drum*. Groups and bands in all combinations sprang up to feed this insatiable (and growing) demand amongst urban Africans for "their" kind of music. Grassroots record companies, like Gallotone, Spades and New Sound, took up the challenge to supply this demand for an authentic African sound. Scouring the music halls, the shebeens and impromptu dance venues, these companies vied to sign the most popular of the current singers and groups. Amongst these performers were groups like the all-girl Gay Gaieties, the all-male The Three Jazzolomos and, probably, the most famous group of all, the harmony group The Manhattan Brothers. Photographs of these stars were regularly printed in the magazine, and torn pages ended up on the walls of the shebeens and music venues. Many of these images were the work of Ian. It enhanced the credibility of the performers to be photographed by someone from *Drum*, especially if that someone was also white, and English.

One of the other staples was the gang culture that was endemic to township life. This was the purview of the African photographers and writers who had grown up in the townships and knew the gang members. Access was a matter of trust.

These tsotsi, the small-time crooks, had been hardened by a tough life and resorted to killing if it got them what they wanted. These gang members believed that they would perish, usually in a blaze of glory having lived a fast life but managing to leave behind "a beautiful corpse". Readers were avid for stories about them and their exploits. Gangs were an aspect of territorial identity. Each township had its gang (sometimes more than one). Sophiatown's most famous gang was called the Americans. Another township had the Russians. These two gangs played out the Cold War, hotly, on the streets of the townships. It became a ritual, a rite of passage, that the various gangs should be pitted against each other. It fell to the *Drum* journalists to record these battles and, sometimes, provide eulogies for the vanquished. Once again, Drum's photographers catered for the curious, though the photographers were always African.

And then there was *King Kong*

"Guess I never realised what a big hit the show was when I was in South Africa. I'd moved on to Paris where it didn't play and I forgot about it."

Ian Berry

From its opening night on 2nd February 1959, in the Wits University Great Hall, Johannesburg, *King Kong*, the musical, was a great success. Ian Berry had moved on to another story by then but his involvement during the rehearsals had produced many wonderful images. Tom Hopkinson saw the coverage of the musical as Ian's chance to experience a long-term and in-depth photo assignment. In a way it was regrettable that, because of work commitments, the cast and crew were able to rehearse in the evenings only. This would put a strain on their free time and on Ian's.

Writing about this aspect of Ian's life in a period so soon after the death of Hugh Masekela, one of the leading musicians of the "orchestra", it is difficult to see that, back then, the international recognition of the power of township music that *King Kong* presaged, could not be foreseen. It is arguable that Paul Simon and his *Graceland* album might not have been possible had not *King Kong* been such a success. Masekela was just one of the musicians who came to prominence during the run of the musical. Ian's photographs would be used later by Mona Glasser in her book: King Kong, a Venture in Theatre.

Part of *King Kong*'s uniqueness was in being an African production. It featured an all-African cast telling an African story about a township boxer with the nickname of King Kong. It charted this boxer's rise and fall and featured songs that underscored elements of the narrative. The music was distinctly township and composed by the Drum journalist Todd Matshikiza.

While Ian's photographs covered every aspect of the rehearsals what they did not cover were the late-night challenges faced by the African cast. Many of them were forced to walk home in the dark, and it was during these night-time walks that they were often harassed by SAP mobile patrols. One night, Kiepe Moeketsi, the township favourite and recording artist was challenged to prove the alto-saxophone he was carrying was his, and not stolen. This Kiepe did by choosing a familiar, Afrikaner folk tune. By three o'clock in the morning the, by-now maudlin, police officers took pity on him and gave Kiepe a lift home in their Black Maria.

Even an inoffensive musical was not free from political overtones. On the opening night, Nelson Mandela thanked Matshikiza for the song, *Sad Times, Bad Times*. which Mandela saw as a reference to the infamous 1956-1961 Treason Trials.

The production was a sell-out at every South African venue where it played. On 23rd February 1961, it opened to packed houses at the Princes Theatre in London. This opening night came less than a year after the shootings in Sharpeville and, by then, people in the UK and beyond were increasingly aware of the scale of the apartheid in South Africa.

Many of South Africa's musicians (and members of the *King Kong* cast), amongst them Miriam Makeba, Hugh Masekela and Todd Mitshikiza, were sent into exile under the Suppression of Communism Act. Music was yet another aspect of life in South Africa that would be seen as subversive! Todd Mitshikiza died in Zimbabwe before the end of apartheid, never having been free to return home.

The Road to Sharpeville

"The native mentality does not allow them to gather for a peaceful demonstration. For them to gather means violence" .

"I don't know how many we shot."

both quotes come from Lieutenant Colonel Pienaar of the South African Police giving evidence to the Judicial Inquiry

If there is one event that marks Ian Berry's transition from a domestic *Drum* photographer to a photojournalist of international renown it is surely the 1960 shootings at Sharpeville, when the South African Police opened fire on an African demonstration. Any hope of keeping the horror of apartheid hidden from the wider world evaporated at that moment. The world looked on aghast as the dead were buried and the authorities seemed not to care.

Ian should not have been there. It was his day off. A telephone call from Tom Hopkinson alerted Ian to the possibility of a story. Tom's alert included the news that someone had already been killed. Being Ian, he was keen to go. The problem was that Peter Magubane was out with *Drum's* only vehicle. The solution was to give Ian the keys to his own car, and assign Drum's assistant editor, Humphrey Tyler to accompany him. With Tom's words of caution about his car ringing in their ears the two journalists drove to Sharpeville as carefully as was possible but as fast as was expedient.

Tension between the Afrikaners and Africans had been growing for a long time. When seven SAP officers were killed at Cato Manor township in January of 1960 a fuse had been lit on a powder keg of mistrust. The default position of the ANC had been to campaign within the law. Their president was Chief Alfred Luthuli, who would later be awarded the Nobel Peace Prize (and be the subject of one of Ian's notable stories). The ANC were well organised and functioned in a similar way to that of a trade union. However, though Chief Luthuli saw 1960 as the year of protest against the Pass Laws, it would be left to PAC members to take direct action. It was their local organisation that called for the demonstration at Sharpeville.

By forcing the SAP to arrest its members, the PAC hoped to clog the judicial process. Africans were restricted to certain areas, which necessitated possessing the appropriate pass. To travel to work out of the prescribed home area required yet another pass. There were curfews and to stay out after curfew required yet more paperwork. Burning these dreaded passes as a protest and a statement of civil disobedience would, it was hoped, create chaos. The 21st March was chosen by PAC for this protest as it pre-empted any planned action by the ANC.

Sharpeville was a manufactured community, the design of which had been influenced by advice from SAP. Its wide streets and the strategic placing of the police station were part of the overall plan to give the authorities the best chance of exerting control and providing the SAP easy access should this be necessary.

Sharpeville, South Africa

Unarmed township people flee the police firing live ammunition. More than 70 were killed and 180 wounded, most shot in the back as they ran. One young boy pulls his coat over his head as if that would protect him from bullets

With a mere two months since the killings at Cato Manor there was a growing sense of paranoia amongst the Afrikaners. There was a firmly held belief amongst them that any anti-government activity by the Africans must be influenced by the communist forces. This was given even more credibility by the influence ofthe American CIA. In his book *Legacy of Ashes, The History of the CIA,* Tim Weiner makes clear the link between the CIA and the South African secret service, BOSS. The pervasive atmosphere of suspicion between East and West became manifest in the CIA's suspicion that all the top members of both ANC and PAC were communists, so much so that Nelson Mandela became a target along with other members of the ANC's hierarchy. SAP officers were influenced by this CIA perception to the point that the "Red Menace" was seen as a real threat.

"If we did not act... the blacks would have killed us and then gone on to slaughter our women and children." This is a comment from a white SAP officer who was at Sharpeville. This fear of a communist-inspired rebellion extended to BOSS's perception of *Drum*. It is hard to imagine Ian Berry as a KGB-trained agent as per Karla from a John Le Carré novel.

On the day of the demonstration, PAC members duly presented themselves at various police stations demanding they be arrested. This was not universal and failed to achieve PAC's goal of bringing the judicial system to a standstill through the simple expedient of overload. However, there was one place where the action was supported. A growing number of people were gathering outside Sharpeville police station.

By the time Ian and Humphrey arrived at the outskirts of Sharpeville, they were met by a large police presence. On the surface everything seemed relaxed and even friendly, so much so that when South African Air Force Sabre jets and Harvard trainers flew low over the gathering (in an attempt to disperse the crowd), the people believed it was a display put on specially for their benefit and they waved excitedly.

Ian's early photographs show a calm, even festive, atmosphere. There was nothing in those early photographs to hint at the horrors to come. The bulk of the press were refused entry and even threatened. Most obeyed the demand and left. This could have been due, in part, to the simple fact that many of these journalists came from outside South Africa.

Ian was now familiar with the way the SAP worked and decided to persist. He followed the unmarked police cars and SAP's Saracen armoured personnel carriers (a British Army vehicle built to withstand small arms fire and mines) along Zwane Street, where the crowds lining the road waved to the police in the APCs. The progress of the Saracens through the township was stately. It culminated inside the fenced enclosure of the police station. This was early afternoon and the heat of the day drove many of the women to find shade beneath their umbrellas. The police featured in those early photographs appear equally relaxed as the crowd remained in a festive mood.

Braving even more angry threats from SAP officers, and using guile, Ian and Humphrey managed to evade the strong police presence for a second time and parked their car out of the way yet close enough to the police station. Out of all the journalists who arrived at Sharpeville, they were the only ones to penetrate the cordon and mingle with the demonstrators.

It has always been a contentious issue as to how many demonstrators were present. Estimates vary from 3,000 to 64,000, depending on who supplies the numbers. As to their mood, Ian had no trouble in moving amongst the crowd. He even reached the fence that surrounded the police station, which was the closest the crowd could come to the SAP. Not only was Ian able to walk freely amongst the crowd: the superintendent of Sharpeville's police detachment was able to walk unmolested through the gathering as he made his way to the police compound. He even stopped to talk with some of the Africans. At the inquest, Ian was challenged about his being able to move freely through the crowd. The police claimed that this was impossible. Ian's reply (under oath) was that he had found it easy enough but had been forced to say *"Excuse me"* on a couple of occasions.

As for the relationship between the Sharpeville SAP contingent and the demonstrators, it was noticeable that, when the number of rounds fired came to be counted, the tally showed that it was the Sharpeville officers who fired the least. The Johannesburg officers had fired by far the most rounds.

Sharpeville, South Africa

A man implores a woman to get up but she is lying dead on the ground, a victim of the police opening fire on an unarmed crowd

Later, as the day wore on and the midday sun continued to beat down upon the crowds gathered around the Sharpeville police compound, there seemed to be no further signs of action. Ian was aware that one of his cameras, the one with the 50mm lens, had very few unexposed frames left on the roll of film. Reloading would take time and, perhaps, not be necessary. Upon returning to the car, he suggested to Humphrey they call it a day. At that point, the sound of gunshots were heard and Ian raced back to see what was happening.

Ian's reaction was *"At first I thought they were shooting blanks!"* It wasn't until people began falling around him and remaining lifeless where they fell that he realised the ammunition was live. A woman standing next to him fell dead. By then Ian had fallen flat on the ground. This gave his subsequent images a unique feel, one of being intimately involved. He was looking up at the people as they were running towards him. These terrified Africans dominate every image. The camera with the 50mm lens was of little use as it needed a fresh roll of film and there had been no time to reload. Ian was, therefore, left with only the camera with the 35mm lens. This meant that, as Ian photographed the chaos that was unfolding in front of him, the area of coverage was wide and included a considerable amount of the background. Asking him to choose an image he feels could tell the story best, he chooses that of a young boy who ran past him trying to shield himself with his coat. Another classic image is of an old man who had stopped to tell a prone figure to get up and run. The old man is talking to a corpse. All these and other iconic images would later show the world the extent of the violence of that day and in so doing change the future of South Africa forever.

When the shooting stopped and silence fell, Ian and Humphrey slipped away, only to become lost in the side streets of Sharpeville. Two men alone in a car, two white men in a township where white men had just killed many Africans surely would lead to retribution. Tentatively, they asked for directions. Ian and Humphrey were surprised when they were helped not only to leave Sharpeville but to be shown a route whereby they avoided the SAP cordon.

The shootings took place on 21st March 1960. By 30th March there were protests and riots throughout the country. The situation across South Africa gave the government permission to declare a state of emergency. Under these new regulations over 18,000 people were arrested. The aftermath of Sharpeville was South Africa's equivalent to Adolf Hitler's Reichstag fire as an excuse for punitive action.

On the 1st April the UN Security Council passed Resolution 134, which voiced the anger of the council and requested the South African government initiate measures to abandon apartheid and work towards racial harmony. Of the members of the council, nine voted in favour whilst only France and the United Kingdom abstained.

There was a Commission of Inquiry at which the SAP evidence was provided by the senior officer present, Lieutenant Colonel Pienaar. It was variously claimed that the demonstrators were armed and aggressive, or had sparked the incident by throwing stones at the police. It was also claimed that a young officer had been pushed over and the crowd moved forward to see what was going on. Whatever the reason, there was no warning that the police would open fire. A later analysis of the ammunition expended revealed that over 1,300 rounds had been fired.

"Jim Bailey wouldn't use the photographs. It was Camera Press who eventually published them. ...I did find that people's perceptions of you changed. Anyone who's been shot at MUST be a good photographer. No. If anything, those photographs of Sharpeville were not very good." This is Ian's verdict.

"It was from then on that Tom (Hopkinson) found his position at Drum *increasingly untenable. The relationship he had with Jim Bailey deteriorated. Tom Hopkinson was a journalist who appreciated photography. Like his predecessors he felt his editorial integrity questioned."*

What were the long-term effects of the shootings? For Ian, it meant international fame and the offer of work from a variety of organisations. This was both fortunate and a disadvantage for Ian. His international fame brought with it an international reputation but, as far as the SAP was concerned, it made him a bigger target.

For South Africa, it was a turning point. Nothing would ever be the same again. The reality of Apartheid was exposed and there could be no going back for the white South Africans. The only way a resolution could be reached was through more violent action.

For Lieutenant Colonel Pienaar, when asked if he had learned anything he replied that "(now he) ...*might be able to get better equipment"*.

To Ian, the importance of his Sharpeville pictures came from the event they recorded, rather than the quality of the images. Ask him about the role he played and he will dissemble and shrink from telling you much. Downplaying his role in the Sharpeville incident he called his "fame" a seven-day wonder. Yet, the name Sharpeville was to reverberate around the world and there could be no hiding from the aftershock. There was little more that Ian could do but be carried along by the consequences of the actions of others. It was the decisions taken by Jim Bailey, the South African police and the national government, that would determine Ian's next move. Tom Hopkinson could see how the situation might play out and helped persuade Ian to leave South Africa and make his way in the wider world.

Ian's photographs were circulating worldwide and there was little the South African Government could do about that. Ian had also given evidence under oath, which embarrassed those in power. It didn't take a fortune-teller to predict the simple fact that the authorities could not tolerate his continued presence in South Africa.

"The way the SAP treated me was making life difficult. I was obviously a rooinek, a term of derision but part of the culture back then. I can honestly say that I never had any trouble with the Africans. Any trouble came from the Afrikaners." Ian Berry

Africa: Congo Independence 1960

"Ian Berry's spectacular success at Sharpeville... coming on top of his winning the Encyclopaedia Britannica award earlier in the year, had made him very hot property indeed. Bombarded with offers from overseas, he naturally asked whether Drum *could increase his all too modest salary."*

Tom Hopkinson

Despite all these accolades, *Drum's* owner still wanted to sack Ian, ostensibly on the grounds of cost. It would be cheaper, Bailey argued, to employ Ian for a couple of picture stories per month as a freelance than employ him full time. Bailey's parsimony had blinded him to the need to employ a full-time photographer who was in possession of a passport. Having a highly regarded English photographer working at *Drum* was not the kudos it might seem. For Bailey, it probably meant this celebrated photographer could well take it into his head to work on stories antipathetic towards the authorities. With his new-found reputation it would mean Ian's images would be snapped up by the editors of the world's media. Without doubt, he would be harder to control and his presence as "The Photographer of Sharpeville" could well result in *Drum* being shut down.

Further north, the Belgian Government moved inexorably towards cutting its ties with Africa. Independence, and all that it entailed, had the makings of a big story.

The official ceremony would see the Belgian King handing power to the Congolese. This would be a story of sufficient interest to attract the world's press. There was no alternative. Ian and Tom Hopkinson packed and left for the Belgian Congo.

Getting to the capital, Leopoldville, was easy enough. There were still plenty of flights. Once there, there was a problem that constantly recurred throughout Ian's professional life: who to see and where to go to obtain the necessary bits of official paper. Under less chaotic circumstances, the people to see would invariably be obvious. The Congo, however, was a country in a state of flux. Having the right pieces of paper might not guarantee a trouble-free stay and access to the best of stories.

Apart from the necessary bits of paper, gaining access to the people who mattered was of more pressing importance. Knowing who counted was paramount. How fortunate then that Tom Hopkinson had a friend in the local *Time-Life* office, its boss Jim Bell. The real problem, according to Bell, was *"Congolese military bloody- mindedness".*

On the eve of independence from Belgium, there was considerable unrest within the Congo. Cracks had existed between the various tribes (and amongst the various interest groups) for some time but had been either ignored or papered over. As independence came closer these cracks became increasingly obvious. Tribal dreams were such that they became a potent rallying cry and their variety merely added to the increased tension on the streets, especially of the capital Leopoldville. The possibility of a power vacuum at the top, once the Belgian authorities left, was all too real. Throughout their time as a colonial power, the Belgian authorities had governed through a European civil service. The country had been a source of employment for Belgian citizens, but not for the local population.

Leopoldville, Congo
King Baudouin II of the Belgians and President Joseph Kasavubu are driven away from the Independence Day ceremony on 30 June 1960

Elisabethville, Katanga, Congo

A decorated ex Belgian soldier at the Final Retreat Ceremony of the Belgians when the new Katanga flag was raised

Little had been done to enable the indigenous Congolese to manage the transition to independence for themselves. Very few Congolese civil servants were available to take over the necessary administrative functions. It was also evident that something as vital as the health service was impoverished. Few Congolese doctors had been trained to staff the hospitals.

The situation was a powder keg. Even the most peaceful of demonstrations could so easily turn violent. Submerged pressures, seismic rumblings of a tribal nature and thwarted ambitions were enough to exacerbate any pre-independence situation. If all this was not sufficient to cause an uneasy loosening of the colonial apron strings, the Congo possessed rich mineral wealth which certain foreign interests were loath to relinquish. Behind the scenes, these foreign companies worked to maintain their prime positions of control.

One of the more overt and obvious flash points was the demand for an independent state for South Kasai. This was a demand made by Albert Kalonji, on behalf of the Baluba tribe. It was Kalonji's long-held hope to create the independent "Diamond State" of South Kasai. Superficially, this appeared to be another manifestation of ancient tribal antagonisms. Behind Kalonji's demand, however, were the machinations of foreign companies reluctant to relinquish such a valuable source of profit. It was easy enough for these vested interests to play upon Albert Kalonji's dreams of greatness. Seeing himself as a *Mulopwe*, (a great tribal chief entitled to rule an independent nation) Kalonji was ripe for manipulation. The sad truth was that South Kasai had little by way of any resources other than diamonds. To sustain the Diamond State, with Kalonji as its chief, would require total commitment from these mining companies, providing everything from water to currency, from food to consumer goods. International companies can be notoriously perfidious and once the mines became uneconomical, or Kalonji's face no longer fitted, these companies could easily abandon their erstwhile "friend".

Soon after Ian Berry and Tom Hopkinson arrived, they heard of a crowd gathering in a part of Leopoldville to listen to a speech by Kalonji. Sniffing a possible story, they went to photograph the demonstration. After a rousing speech from the back of a lorry, Kalonji disappeared. *"Suddenly, a jeep in the square began to move. It ran rapidly up the road towards the crowd [those who had gathered to listen to Kalonji] and a Congolese soldier standing in the back began to fire. He was not firing directly at the crowd, but lobbing canisters which turned over and over in the air and then fell, hissing, amongst their feet. Clouds of smoke fizzed out of every canister... 'They're using tear gas!' he [Ian] thrust his camera bag into my hands, tied a handkerchief round his nose, dodged past the soldiers in the square and disappeared up the road into the trouble."* Tom Hopkinson

Hopkinson tried three times to follow Ian but each time he was driven back by the smoke.

"Ian, slight, bearded, diffident, was in his element when there was trouble. Tom Hopkinson

The gathering of photographers in the Congo allowed Tom Hopkinson to meet some of the other photographers working in Africa. One such is featured on a photograph of the limousine carrying King Baudouin of Belgium and the newly appointed President Kasavubu. This is Larry Burrows, there on assignment for *Life Magazine*. Burrows would become famous for his award-winning coverage of the Vietnam War, where his life was to be cut short in 1971, killed when the helicopter he was travelling in was shot down. There was also Barry von Below, who worked for the *Johannesburg Star*, and another South African, Ernie Christie.

The sight of this quartet trying to outrun King Baudouin and President Kasavubu's limousine caused Tom Hopkinson some degree of amusement. Ernie Christie had been a footballer and ran easily enough. Barry von Below had problems; whilst Ian ran with a *"High, loping stride"* and Larry Burrows looked *"...ready to drop",* but managed to hold on.

Turning and taking the occasional picture, the quartet obtained a lift in a lorry that was preceding the royal limousine. Whilst the lift no doubt saved the four of them from exhaustion, it meant they missed the most iconic image, that of Ambroise Boimbo running alongside the Presidential limousine and stealing King Baudouin's ceremonial sword. This photograph was captured by a German photographer, Max Scheler

Some time later Tom Hopkinson received a single-word message, the name of a place, *Dendala*! Dendala was a suburb of Leopoldville. It was also almost exclusively home to the Bakongo people. The Bakongo tribe were an influential group and had helped secure the presidency for Joseph Kasavubu.

With Ian and Barry von Bulow sharing his taxi, Tom Hopkinson travelled to Dendala. It was Sunday and everywhere looked peaceful enough. Couples were walking, seemingly out for a stroll in the sun, and children were playing. However, the further they drove into the suburb the streets filled with more and more people.

Along with the growing crowds, there was an increasingly heightened sense of tension; a palpable feeling that something was about to happen. Here and there piles of tyres had been set on fire; their acrid smoke drifting skyward in the heat and adding their stench to this feeling of foreboding.

It was Ian who noticed the action and its potential.

"A big, powerfully built fellow in a white, sleeveless vest was running through the crowd, pounding slowly but determinedly like a rugby player through a crowd of would-be tacklers. His pursuers dodged after him, slashing and beating, some with sticks or strips of rubber cut from car tyres; one or two with iron bars, and everyone, as they saw him coming, joined in with whatever was handy – some even slipping off their shoes to crack at him...."
Tom Hopkinson

Ian immediately left the taxi, as the man came towards him. The crowd continued to beat the man, who fell down in front of Ian whilst Ian continued to take his pictures. Tom rushed out of the taxi, stood over the man shouting at the aggressive crowd. This pause in the assault gave the victim a chance to stagger off round the corner.

Though Hopkinson's intervention gave the victim a chance to escape, it placed both Hopkinson and Ian in a vulnerable position especially exposing Ian to retribution him being a photographer. Half in jest, Ian turned to Tom and said *"If you ever do something as damn silly as that again, don't do it with my exposed film in your pocket."*

Only later, when Ian had a chance to reflect upon the events of the day, was the moral significance of the scene become apparent: *"At what point should a photographer stop taking pictures and interfere with events."*

Later on in his career (in Northern Ireland), a similar incident caused him to face an even more complicated dilemma.

Katanga

Two days after returning to Johannesburg, news came through from the Congo that there was a full-scale revolt by the *Force Publique.* It had been obvious during their previous trip to the Congo that this well-armed, semi-military force of about 24,000 Gendarmes would do all that they could to seek greater powers once Independence became a reality.

As if the Force Publique flexing its muscles wasn't trouble enough, Albert Kalonji was still agitating for an independent South Kasai. But now it was not only Kalonji who was seeking independence. The larger and wealthier region of Katanga also demanded independence. In 1960, the President of Katanga's Provincial Legislature, Moise Tshombe, took the fateful step of declaring Katanga an independent country.

In many ways Katanga was similar to South Kasai in that it was mineral rich. However, its economic importance lay in its copper and cobalt mines, rather than in diamonds. As with South Kasai, Katanga had attracted the interest of mining companies. Because its ambitions for independence coincided with the interests of several Belgium companies, these corporations supported Tshombe's ambitions. To those in Leopoldville, it was clear that the independence of Katanga, in particular, would reduce the economic viability of the rest of the Congo. The hope had been that the Congo could remain united. The then Prime Minister of the Congo, Patrice Lumumba, opposed any move towards the independence of both Katanga and South Kasai. With such obdurate and irreconcilable African parties at loggerheads, the back stage machinations by European companies not only exacerbated an already volatile situation but they were in a position to (covertly) add their financial muscle to the mix. If all that wasn't enough, there was a growing belief (especially in the USA) that Lumumba was a Communist. A tragedy of Shakespearean proportions was playing itself out in twentieth century Africa.

Elisabethville, Katanga, Congo

Most Katangese soldiers fighting the UN carry automatic weapons but some continue to carry their bows and arrows

Ian's photographs from the independence celebrations had proved bestsellers, both in South Africa and abroad. There was a demand for more. Once again, both he and Tom Hopkinson travelled north; this time to Katanga. Now, though, the journey was not so straightforward. Getting to Katanga was proving to be very difficult. There were no direct flights and travelling to Leopoldville was a non-starter. Therefore, the journey would be have to be by a circuitous route through Northern Rhodesia (now Zambia).

Upon arrival at the Rhodesian border town of Ndola they found it full to overflowing with refugees. While they waited to travel onwards, Ian wandered amongst the groups of displaced people and photographed them. Eventually, Ian and Tom were able to continue their journey onwards and flew to Elisabethville, (renamed Lubumbashi in 1960).

The airport at Elisabethville was as full of refugees as Ndola had been, if not more so. The big difference between the two towns lay in the state of confusion and chaos that had caused so much disruption to the authorities. *"All customs and immigration services had broken down; arriving passengers collected their own luggage and looked around for some means getting into town."* Tom Hopkinson

All the signs were of a town where the last vestiges of civil control were breaking down. Every system upon which any international airport depends, from the customs and immigration services to mundane functions such as refreshments and hygiene and public safety, were no longer in evidence.

The airport was a scene of inaction. After photographing the Belgian paratroopers digging in and setting up a defensive perimeter there was little else to do. Any news that came from the official sources was bland and sanitised. It was decided that Tom and Ian would walk into town. This turned out to be a brave move, if somewhat foolhardy. The rebellious gendarmerie picked them up. Thankfully, Tom Hopkinson was sufficiently fluent in French to initiate a conversation with their captors. Having put them at their ease and convinced them they were neither Belgian spies nor were they Belgian soldiers in disguise, the conversation became more of an interview where Tom was hearing the "other side" of the story and Ian was about to take photographs. This was the moment when a patrol of Belgian Paratroopers arrived to make a dashing, but unnecessary, rescue.

Back in Elisabethville and leaving the airport clutter behind, Ian and Tom went in search of somewhere safe from which to work – the hotel which was the one favoured by the other journalists covering the civil war.

A curfew was imposed at night and armed guards took over the post office and the radio station. Undaunted, Ian and Tom walked the deserted streets searching for the Provincial House where, it was rumoured, a meeting was to take place. Whether there was a meeting or not, they never discovered. Instead, they were arrested yet again.

The two men were taken to the central police headquarters. Walking through the station court yard, they found it full of arrested looters and a large stockpile of stolen goods. Thankfully, for both Ian and Tom's sakes, a Belgian officer was on hand to help resolve the situation. Freed, they returned to the hotel. Though safe for the time being, their journalistic curiosity remained unsatisfied.

In Jadotville (now Likasi), they witnessed the violent disintegration of Congolese society. Arriving in the town, this disintegration was personified by the fate of a jeweller. Through his tears, he pointed to the ruin of his shop. 6,000,000 Francs worth of goods had been stolen leaving him with only a million Francs worth of stock left. However, as he pointed out, that this was made up mainly of grandfather clocks and fish knives which, he lamented, he had been unable to sell so far and would not be able to sell in the future. No one wanted to buy fish knives or grandfather clocks and the looters were canny enough to realise this.

Back in Elisabethville they found the number of prisoners had mushroomed! The need for places of confinement had meant the authorities were forced to requisition a sports ground in which to hold them. Ian took the opportunity to photograph the inmates.

Moving on to the airport, Ian and Tom found that the situation was even more chaotic than when they had left to go to Jadotville. Now, it had been necessary to commandeer one of the aircraft hangers to house yet more prisoners. Various rumours abounded, adding to the confusion and creating an atmosphere of fear and suspicion. Seeking answers to their many questions, Tom and Ian felt it necessary to attend the daily 3pm press conference held by Tshombe at his villa.

Moise Tshombe had proclaimed himself President of the State of Katanga, and in so doing had effectively deprived the newly independent Congo of 50% of its revenue. In an effort to regain this, the Congolese Prime Minister Patrice Lumumba sought the help of the United States and the United Nations. All this had taken place within a week of Katanga's unilateral declaration of independence. The reality on the ground was that Belgian forces were supporting the Katangese rebellion. The situation was under consideration at the UN and these deliberations resulted in Security Council Resolution 143 which called for the immediate removal of Belgian forces and the deployment of UN troops in Katanga.

The unrest continued. In America, the President Eisenhower was on holiday and unable to meet Lumumba. Instead Lumumba met the US Secretary of State, Christian Herter, who confirmed the USA's position that they would only intervene as part of a larger UN effort.

To further complicate matters South Kasai chose this moment to announce that it, too, was breaking away from the Congo. Lumumba's reaction was to send in troops to retake South Kasai. For Lumumba, this was a very logical move. Should there be any future action taken against Katanga it would necessitate the movement of troops by rail. The rail link to Katanga passed through South Kasai.

There was always the problem of tribal allegiance. This had exacerbated the distrust the president of the Congo, Kasavubu, felt towards Lumumba, the prime minister. Kasavubu also resented Lumumba's increasingly significant contacts with the Soviet bloc. This had led Kasavubu to believe Lumumba was creating a parallel state.

In and around Leopoldville the ethnic divisions were becoming markedly more extreme. The Catholic Church criticised Lumumba and his government; the UN forces, by then patrolling Katanga, were making a difference but only just. Their presence had not crushed the rebellion as Lumumba had hoped. In the meantime, the bid for independence by South Kasai had been violently put down by Congolese forces under the command of Joseph Mobutu, a former soldier.

Tshombe took the opportunity to announce that President Lumumba had approached communist sources asking for help. This was cleverly timed as, considering the state of the world in 1960, even the suspicion of turning this part of West Africa into a sphere of Soviet influence was unacceptable to both the Pentagon and the White House. Unfortunately, these assertions turned out to be true. Lumumba had approached the Soviet Premier Nikita Khrushchev, asking for help.

Leopoldville (Kinshasa), Congo
A man of a different tribe is being pursued and stoned by a mob shortly after independence

With this as a bargaining chip, Tshombe sought aid and recognition from the United States, using Lumumba's "communist" connection as leverage. Lumumba had wanted to avoid taking sides and hoped for aid and support from the West. That was now impossible and the die was cast. Lumumba, as far as the CIA was concerned, was a marked man.

Whether Lumumba was a communist or not did not matter. As far as President Kasavubu was concerned, he believed that Lumumba would mount a coup and take sole control of the government. In the hope of preventing this he sacked Lumumba and six other ministers. Lumumba was not dismissed in a face-to-face meeting. Instead, he heard the news of his dismissal in a radio broadcast on the evening of 5th September. Outraged, Lumumba went to the national radio station, forced his way past the UN guards, took to the air to denounce his dismissal as illegal and that Kasavubu was the traitor and not him. Once that was made public in the broadcast Lumumba declared it was Kasavubu who would be deposed.

The Katangese Rebel Army, which took to the field, was a ragtag collection of Katanga natives and mercenaries. Ian's photographs capture the ad hoc nature of this army exemplified by their attire and tactics. The soldiers he photographed are in their baggy jackets and ancient shorts, seen-better-days bush hats, and armed with their old British bolt action Lee Enfields, possibly of 1914 vintage. In one of his pictures a group of them are caught sheltering from a heavy rain storm in Elisabethville. What is implicit in Ian's photographs is the lack of discipline, the unpredictable nature of these soldiers and their potential for extreme violence.

The Congo and its conflicts became a "hot" news item, and Ian's work was more and more in demand by the international market. Ian photographed the fighting in and around Elisabethville. If you were unarmed and white this was a dangerous time to be seen anywhere in Katanga without a military escort. Leaving a hostelry after a heavy session of liquid refreshment, a German mercenary chose to open fire on Ian and his two companions. Fortunately, he was too inebriated for his shots to be accurate. Failing to kill the white photographers and having emptied his magazine, the drunken soldier departed, but not before a group of near-by Katangese troops witnessed the shooting.

Putting two and two together and making five, the Katangese soldiers decided to finish the job the German had started. Meanwhile, Ian, believing the departure of the German had put an end to the incident continued to photograph the detritus left by the conflict. At this point the Katangese soldiers chose to intervene and a chase ensued.

Though young and active, Ian and two other photographers thought it best to seek sanctuary in a nearby block of flats, discretion being the better part of valour. After trying first one door and then the next, their efforts were to no avail. Not one of the Belgian residents was prepared to open their door. It was hardly surprising given the circumstances. Their pleas fell on deaf ears. The reluctance of the Belgian inhabitants of the flats to become involved gave Ian some indication of what could happen.

Cornered, and with no possible means of escape, there was little alternative but to surrender to the Katangese. Ian, as was his customary positive cheerfulness, hoped to be able to talk his way out of any trouble. It had worked in the past and would do so again in future situations But not this time.

The Katangese troops refused to listen, assuming they understood what was being said to them. A nearby wall would suffice for the execution. Ian says that even now he is aware that the rush of adrenalin and the speed at which the events were playing out, meant that even when the soldiers formed up into a firing squad the surreal nature of the situation robbed it of much of its menace. There were no onlookers to witness what was going to happen, nor was there any possibility of escape. There was to be no ceremony, no final cigarette or offer of a blindfold.

South Africa's black youth had a saying *"Live fast, die young and leave a good-looking corpse."* How ironic it would be if this was to be Ian's epitaph. Ian is still philosophical on the subject of death. During one of our recent sessions, he told me that dying young was good for a photographer's CV. To be an old photographer robbed you of much of the glamour. It would be obvious to one and all that the situations you found yourself in were not that dangerous. They couldn't be. You had survived.

With the Katangese squad on the lookout for spies, you would have thought they would know what to do next. Not so. As Ian looked on, what had passed for coherence amongst the troops slowly descended into chaos as first one of the soldiers and then another put forward their own view of what to do next. In a very Marxist way each member of the firing squad had an opinion and expressed it vociferously. After all, these white men might be spies for Lumumba or the Belgians, or even not spies but what they said they were. It was all very confusing.

Before any consensus could be arrived at, a Rhodesian mercenary arrived and resolved the matter. After quickly assessing the situation, this Rhodesian knight in a sweaty khaki uniform spoke with the chief of the Katangese, telling him he was taking over and would take their catch with him to see the president. The mention of Tshombe's name worked wonders and the rifles were lowered. However, this meant a trip to the home of the President, Tshombe.

Now that the threat of the firing squad had passed, an audience with the self- proclaimed president of Katanga might result in a similar outcome. Off they went to the president's palace and into the presence of the man himself. There could be no predicting what might happen. It could well be another firing squad, or a dank prison cell. Instead, when Ian and his companions were introduced to President Tshombe, he offered them tea and biscuits.

For many of the photojournalists who travelled the world to capture the truth, their lives veer between fear, tragedy and farce. Civil war is, perhaps, the most intimate of any war and usually prosecuted with extreme violence. Everything is up close and very personal. There is often little or no scope for the modern style of waging war, with drones and laser-guided munitions. Death in its many manifestations is "in your face".

Questioning Ian about this and asking where the photographer's place is on the battlefield, he is somewhat sanguine. He sees the likes of Don McCullin or James Nachtway as war photographers, the best. They are very focused upon the ebb and flow of a battle and have an affinity with the smell of cordite. Ask Ian about his good friend Philip Jones Griffiths, and the classic book *Vietnam Inc*, he shares Henri Cartier-Bresson's view of him: *"He (Philip) was not the best war photographer but the best photographer of war."*

Yet, Ian has been close to conflict in its many forms and recorded death in its many guises: from shootings like Sharpeville to the East African famines and those murdered by the horrendous method of "necklacing". This is a South African method of killing which involves placing tyres around the victim's neck and setting them alight. He has photographed conflict in Vietnam and in Israel, yet he maintains that his work is not that of a war photographer.

The UN in the Congo

With Ian's increasingly important profile, doors were opening for him. Those last months in Congo and Katanga saw Ian accompanying the UN presence. This happy co-operation led to some of Ian's most perceptive and memorable work: for example, the look upon the face of the young Swedish soldier as he attempts to supervise the distribution of food. It is not only the expression on his face but the tense way he holds his Carl Gustaf machine gun.

The convoluted history of the Congo in all its manifestations is really not part of our story. Suffice to say that the United Nations became involved and, with the encouragement of the UN Secretary General Dag Hammarskjöld, UN troops arrived to bring order in place of chaos and reduce the killing. Ian spent time travelling with the UN, making a pictorial record of their policing. These various forays often provided good photo opportunities, along with a chance to sample international cuisine and, sometimes, the odd surprise. Ian was with the UN official Conor Cruise O'Brien when O'Brien and his party came under fire from an aircraft. Ian captured the moment when the party fell flat to avoid being killed. To make the shot Ian must have sat up exposing his body to the strafing aircraft.

It was whilst out with a Swedish officer travelling around the various posts controlled by the UN, that Ian and the officer heard what sounded like a firefight. Multiple shots and explosions came from somewhere nearby. Driving hastily to the scene and expecting to witness combat, both Ian and the Swedish UN officer were bemused to discover desperate action, certainly, but not enemy action. They were in an area patrolled by Irish UN troops (Elisabethville) who had established a sizeable camp. Driving into the camp Ian managed to capture several spectacular action shots, especially of the chaos caused by the explosions. Troopers were running back and forth carrying shells to safety, away from the conflagration. To this day Ian has no idea what caused the Irish ammunition dump to catch fire. He suspects someone might have been getting out of the way for a crafty cigarette but there is no concrete evidence one way or another. Stored on site were expended shells which should have been inert but, because they contained a modicum of explosive material, were potentially still dangerous.

Thankfully, these explosions caused very little damage. The troops, however, were nevertheless suitably disconcerted and initially believed they were under fire. Apart from offering a chance to make dramatic photographs, Ian was fond of visiting the Irish troops as they invariably offered him not only a decent cup of tea but also a slice of homemade cake. Sad to say when with the Swedish troops Ian was treated to fruit juice and salad.

One of Ian's wishes was to photograph the Gurkhas fighting in Elisabethville. He approached the officer in charge of the detachment, a Sandhurst Military College trained Sikh. It was agreed that Ian would report back that night and go with the unit as they rid the post office of the Katangese rebels who were hiding in it. Waiting in the dark with the officer, Ian was aware that using a flash would be a non-starter. Instead, he was hoping to have enough light provided by the fire fight and the explosives.

The two men waited. There was nothing but silence and ever-deepening darkness.

Finally, a soldier informed them that the job was done. No flash-bangs? Apparently not. On entering the post office the bodies of the Katangese rebels were scattered over the floor, each one silently killed by the Gurkhas use of the Kukri. Every rebel's' throat had been clinically cut.

Elisabethville, Katanga, Congo
The first of the UN Moroccan soldiers arrive by train from a different part of the Congo

Africa never quite finished with Ian. Perhaps it might be more accurate to say that Ian never quite finished with Africa. Of the stories he tells, other than those already recounted, there is one which Ian relates that caused a problem, in that it upset the delicate natural balance of events. One of *Life* magazine's women photographers came to South Africa to cover a story about African mine workers fighting amongst themselves. On the face of it, it would appear to be an example of inter-tribal violence. These fights took place over the weekends and were seen as spectator sport by the whites rather than anything more serious. But, when the photographs were processed and turned into a story they were seen as *"terrible events... the white mine owners make their workers fight, along ethnic and tribal lines".* Ian Berry

The natural consequence was that the mine owners stopped the "official" weekend fighting. Sad to say the fighting did not end. It became a matter of tribal honour to continue these matches and, now being unofficial, the results could be frightening. A tribe's prestige could be won or lost on the dusty battle ground. Should a fighter from one of the minor tribes win, the result could be an enormous free-for-all with serious casualties all round.

On another occasion, whilst standing on the meagre airport that served Basutoland (which became the Kingdom of Lesotho in 1966), Ian waited with the local hierarchy for the aircraft carrying Harold Wilson, the British prime minister to land. This was the time when MacMillan was travelling throughout Africa with his "Winds of Change" speech.

Elisabethville, Katanga, Congo

Irish UN soldiers, who thought they were under attack in their camp, rescue ammunition from their exploding dump, possibly set off by a stray cigarette

The plane landed and the assembled party made ready to greet MacMillan. Lady MacMillan walked towards the gathered dignitaries. Not so her husband. Prime Minister MacMillan stormed off with great determination towards the bushes that surrounded the air strip. Believing that the British Prime Minister wanted to relieve himself, the reception committee waited, unsure quite what to do. It was Ian who caught up with him, took hold of his arm and pointed the myopic Prime Minister towards the waiting crowd. It transpired that Harold MacMillan was too vain to wear glasses.

A somewhat similar incident happened in Yugoslavia when Ian was there to photograph President Tito. This was in 1974, late in Tito's career, and Ian was granted only the briefest of accesses. The situation had the potential to become something richly visual: Tito going on a bear hunt.

Arriving at the start of the hunt, Tito was greeted by the locals who provided a lavish celebratory lunch. After much joviality and back-slapping, Tito made ready for the hunt. Being provided with his loaded gun he looked every inch a star. For full effect, Ian moved in front of the president to taker a classic shot. His camera raised, his finger on the shutter button, Ian was dragged out of the way. It transpired that Tito, like MacMillan, was as blind as a bat and also too vain to wear glasses in public.

On other occasions Ian accompanied the British Royal Family on their tours of the continent. One of his favourites was following Her Royal Highness, Elizabeth the Queen Mother. On this particular day the agenda was set to take the Queen Mother round a factory. There were only a handful of photographers there that day and Ian took the opportunity to climb up on a chair to capture a different shot. As he took the picture the Queen Mother turned to him and said *"What's the problem Ian? Your flash not working?"*

Elisabethville, Katanga, Congo
Irish UN soldiers thinking they have come under fire in their camp rush to avoid flying bullets as their own ammunition dump explodes. It was most probably caused by a stray cigarette

The Queen's visit to Ghana in 1961 was not the propaganda success it might have been. It was obvious that she was unhappy and for the final event the Prime Minister, Kwame Nkrumah hosted a formal ball. There, on the dancefloor, was Her Majesty dancing with Nkrumah. Ian took to the dance floor, staying in front of the couple. Unbeknown to him Prince Phillip (The Duke of Edinburgh) was standing immediately behind him. Ian stepped on Prince Philip's foot. After the initial howl, Prince Philip, having served in the Royal Navy, resorted to a string of expletives. At this point, Ian noticed Her Majesty smiling and captured the moment.

Paris Match ran with this image, their captions being along the lines of *"The only smile of the trip", and "Finally, Her Majesty smiles".*

If 1968 wasn't a year full of events and contrasts, it was also the year when the Miss Europe beauty contest should have been held in Paris. This was thought to be dangerous with the city full of rioting students. For some reason, the contest was to be held in the Congo.

Having arrived from Prague after four days of not eating or sleeping much, Ian was advised by Russ Melcher, the bureau chief to relax for a few days and the beauty contest might be an amusing diversion. It was at this point Ian found that his fellow Magnum photographers were roaming the Paris streets capturing the essence of the riots and there he was accompanying scantily clad women in the baking Equatorial heat of Africa.

Travel was provided in the shape of a chartered plane. This was loaded with contestants, their various entourages and a cohort of accompanying photographers, not to mention the presence of the ubiquitous chaperones. Needless to say the plane's cabin was somewhat cramped.

Upon arrival, each of the contestants was provided with their individual thatched hut, and every hut was provided with its own flagpole suitably flying the national flag of the contestant residing within. This "invasion" of scantily clad, attractive white women caused problems for the local males. Their reactions were very physical and offered many photo opportunities for capturing a clash of cultures. In the end it became a *Carry On* film.

Out of Africa

The time had come for Ian to leave Africa. Ian's mentor, Tom Hopkinson, was finding his tenure as editor of *Drum* intolerable under the aegis of Jim Bailey. In those heady days of the early 1960s, the place to be, the centre of the photojournalists' world, was Paris. With a letter of introduction to Magnum's Henri Cartier-Bresson and words of good-will ringing in his ears, Ian Berry left South Africa for Paris.

At first, Ian worked for a small photo agency opened by an erstwhile Magnum administrator, Michel Chevalier. This was VISA photos which employed a handful of European photographers. Then Magnum approached Ian and asked him if he wanted to join them. It was soon after Ian left VISA that the agency folded, following the sudden and unfortunate death of Chevalier.

Come time to meet Cartier-Bresson, Ian arrived at the venue, a café-bar close to Magnum Photos' Paris office. Believing every Frenchman would drink coffee, Ian ordered coffee. Cartier-Bresson ordered tea. Ian had brought several carefully chosen prints, which he offered to Cartier-Bresson who flicked through the prints and then left.

Bemused by the great man's reaction and somewhat taken aback, Ian sought advice, to be told that Cartier-Bresson favoured studying a person's contact sheets. This, Ian was told, gave Cartier-Bresson a better understanding and insight into how the photographer worked. Aware now of what to do, a second meeting was arranged and this time Ian brought contact sheets and drank tea. With Cartier-Bresson's invitation Ian became an associate of Magnum.

No sooner had Ian been formally accepted by Magnum Photos than he went to photograph the wedding party of Magnum's Inge Morath, who had married the American playwright Arthur Miller. From small beginnings...

*"I joined Magnum so I didn't have to go and see editors and what have you. I'm not good at it. Meeting editors and getting oneself known was all part of what we have to do. Eve (*Arnold*) was very good at this, inviting editors to dinner.... that was the way it was done. In Paris, I remember* Paris Match *and other photo magazines were in the same building. I remember going up in the lift with the then bureau chief Russ (*Melcher*) with a story. We had the pix to show to the* Paris Match *editor, and the editor of* Photo Magazine *got into the same lift. He asked to take a look and tried to outbid* Paris Match *on the way up. We have lost that immediacy".*
Ian Berry

Back in Europe, Ian found life could be just as hectic and unpredictable as in Africa, but in a different way. Those early stories took him all over Europe and even back to Africa. When he worked for *Drum* it meant becoming familiar with one house style and one editor. Now, he was working for many of the most prestigious publications in the world. To that end he photographed the Spanish city of Toledo for *Paris Match*, and the diamond mines of South West Africa and Tanzania for *The Sunday Times*, and in 1962 Ian found himself back in Johannesburg on a story for the *National Geographic Society* about drive-in cinemas.

However, being based in France meant much of his work was in Europe. Stories came thick and fast and through his competition with the rest of the European (and often world's) press Ian learned a good many lessons. One of his earliest stories was to photograph the wedding of the French singer Edith Piaf. It introduced Ian to the potential violence and unremitting competitiveness of the world's press. This was his blooding to the competitive world of the paparazzi. While Ian did manage to capture some worthwhile images he emerged from the ceremony only to discover that his clothing had been torn and some of his equipment was missing. Though this wasn't to be his customary type of story, he was to face something similar a little later, and once again that was in France.

The Jean Cocteau, the renowned French philosopher and author, died of a heart attack at his home in Milly-la-Forét. With one of those coincidences that feature in Greek plays, those where the gods manipulate the lives of humankind, Cocteau's great friend, the singer Edith Piaf, died the day before him but her death was only announced on the morning Cocteau died.

Cocteau wished to be buried beneath the floor of the Chapelle Saint-Blaise des Simples in Milly-la-Forét, close to the altar. Arriving with time to spare (having prior experience of the French press corp) Ian carefully chose his position at the far side of the grave. This would give him a superb view of the coffin and the pallbearers as they walked down the aisle to the author's last resting place. This position was so good that other photographers sought to stake a claim to a part of it. The trouble arose when too many of them crowded in behind Ian. With the coffin and mourners slowly, inexorably approaching, Ian struggled to keep himself from falling forward. Impossible! With the mourners only yards away, Ian felt the final push and tumbled, head-first into the open grave together with several other photographers.

All this happened in 1963. In those early years, there was so much happening and Ian was constantly active. With his growing reputation, Ian worked on story after story, including one about the French President, Charles de Gaulle. Knowing the general's antipathy towards the British, this was felt to be a great honour.

Assigned to the American magazine *Newsweek* to photograph Colonel Nasser, then President of Egypt, Ian flew to Cairo. Nasser had become an icon of Arab nationalism having wrested control of Egypt from the monarchy in 1952 and nationalising the Suez Canal in 1956. Ian was told to wait by the phone in his hotel room for a call that would inform him of a few free minutes in Nasser's busy schedule.

While Ian was waiting patiently, he received a phone call from the picture editor asking that he try to photograph the president on a camel. A second phone call suggested he photograph Colonel Nasser not only on a camel but, if at all possible, on a camel in front of the pyramids. When the call from Nasser's office came Ian was afforded a generous five minutes to photograph the colonel in his office.

Ian found his globetrotting often involved photographing the political giants of the age. One of those stories featured the American President John F Kennedy, on Kennedy's visit to the Pope in Rome. Adding to his collection of senior statesmen and presidents, Ian (then in Africa) answered a request from the German magazine *Neue Illustrierte* (1948 - 1966), to photograph the Conrad Adenauer, German Chancellor. Ian arrived in Germany wearing casual clothing suited for the African heat, and with nothing formal.

Ian usually shot in black and white Ilford film, but the Adenauer assignment meant shooting colour. It was to be Conrad Adenauer's last year in office and considering how long the German Chancellor had been involve fed in politics Ian looked for a fresh approach.

The session proceeded along the customary lines with Adenauer in his office. It was somewhat formal and not to Ian's liking. However, Ian had discovered the Chancellor was an avid gardener and loved roses. Suggesting they retire to the garden, Ian set about photographing Adenauer amongst his roses.

All this was conducted through an interpreter, on Adenauer's insistence. A man of formality and protocol ,Adenauer became more relaxed standing next to his beloved roses, wearing his blue hat. Knowing that was when the shoot had come alive, Ian captured the moment and then thanked the Chancellor and made to leave. It was at this point that Adenauer said, in perfect English: *"German roses are better than English roses."*

In December of that year, Ian was in Berlin to photograph the Christmas truce when the East German Government allowed movement from East to West for families divided by the Wall. This was a momentous event, with the Wall being opened for only a brief while. As Ian stood waiting for the moment when the waiting relatives would be allowed into East Berlin, he tried to talk to some of those who were waiting to cross over. It was whilst moving amongst these relatives that he noticed a man, standing alone. Soberly dressed with a dark overcoat, hat and gloves, this man was the clone of one of the those waiting on the other side of the Wall. Following a hunch, Ian remained close and, sure enough, the two men moved towards each other. It was this photograph, of the two brothers rushing to greet each other with their arms outstretched, that became an iconic image of that Christmas truce. However, Ian (with his customary self-criticism) feels that there is a better photograph, one he took inside an East German guard room where, in one of the corners, stood a small Christmas tree which, at the time, struck Ian as an anomaly, something so unexpected in a so-called communist country.

The experiences of those who lived in the 1960s could, by a stretch of the imagination, place you in one of two camps. There are those who saw the decade as one of LSD, *"Peace and Love.... man!"* and the song *House of the Rising Sun*. However, there are those whose experiences are very different. For this group, their views of the decade were less hedonistic and shaped by a sense of freedom and of experiencing the new. It was a time when (in the words of JFK) they didn't seek to know what our country could do for them but what we could do for our country. It was the decade in which Voluntary Service Overseas and the Peace Corps were born. It was a period of exploration and new horizons. British photographers were hot property. Better known later as *The Young Meteors*, the likes of Philip Jones Griffiths, Don McCullin, Terence Donovan and Tony Armstrong-Jones were breaking new ground and filling the pages of the Sunday supplements. British photojournalism stepped into the limelight. The book which explains this explosion of talent and recognition is *Young Meteors, British Photojournalism: 1957-1965*, by Martin Harrison. Harrison makes mention of Ian's arrival in Britain in the book.

Leaving Paris for a post as the first contract photographer for the *Observer Magazine* suited Ian.

"Paris had been good for me until the last moment." Going out on a limb in 1963, he had chartered a twin-engined plane to fly from Beirut to Baghdad to photograph the Iranian coup d'état. Regrettably, as he flew over Baghdad airport it was blocked with trucks and other vehicles. Ian was forced to fly back to Beirut. Next day, with other photographers joining him on the charter, he tried again. This time he was able to land but he was reduced to watching the events on his hotel television because the coup was over. Seriously out of pocket and with no way of recouping his outlay, the offer of a secure job in London made wonderful sense.

It was during this period of his life that Ian made one of his firm friendships. Philip Jones Griffith was already making a name for himself as a photojournalist when the two men met in Germany. It was Philip Jones Griffith who provided Ian and his pregnant wife with accommodation when they moved from Paris to London.

Working for the *Observer* provided Ian with a world of opportunities, with thirty-four (or thereabouts) stories a year becoming the norm. It was very much a case of *"have passport, will travel".* One week he could find himself travelling to Berlin and the next he could be jetting off to Ghana.

Portraits

"I don't do landscapes.... but I do do people."

Ian Berry

For those who know Ian Berry's work as a documentary photojournalist, it sometimes comes as a surprise when seeing his portrait work for the first time. Whilst working on stories with the *Observer*, Ian photographed a wide range of people. Whilst we've already mentioned his efforts on behalf of *Newsweek* to photograph President Nasser, it should be understood portraits run through Ian's work like a gold thread through a tapestry.

Politics can be fascinating and Ian has the uncanny ability to put the politicians at ease. Some of his recent shoots have covered British General Elections and the 2016 European Referendum. He accompanied some of the politicians as they canvassed during the 2017 election. One was to be Jeremy Corbyn, the then leader and then, as if by chance, he was in Salisbury when the Conservative Minister Priti Patel campaigned there.

Always ready to look beyond the facade deployed by many of the politicians, Ian has a preferred way of working. Time spent with them, listening and capturing moments of some import, Ian has been able to provide an invaluable record of this country's political narrative. During the 1966 election Ian followed Barbara Castle, the Labour firebrand, and captured her attempts to woo the voters. One of his images is an evocation of electioneering as it used to be in the pre-digital age. Mrs Castle is photographed from behind as she stands upon a chair to address an audience of one. The elderly lady comes close to Mrs Castle and has a personal conversation with the politician, emphasising a point with her finger. There is something very raw and unsophisticated about the black and white images from 1966, especially when compared

France
Writer Lawrence Durrell tests a bowl of hot soup in the kitchen of his country house

with the well-oiled campaigns of Corbyn and Patel, with their army of aides to protect them.

Politics aside, Ian was often called upon to photograph celebrities in an age when the title "celebrity" meant something. To quote one example, the South African heart transplant surgeon Dr Christian Barnard, and the recipient of the second transplanted heart both featured in one of Ian's stories.

Whilst working on an annual report for Reuters, Ian went hither and thither around the world photographing various Reuter-linked people. One of these luminaries was the newspaper magnate Robert Maxwell. This was to be a colour shot made indoors. Ian and his assistant set the lighting in an appropriate room and waited. After the passing of the appointed hour, Ian sought clarification and was told to come back in two days' time.

Once again, Ian and his assistant returned to ready the room. Once again, Maxwell did not turn up. With no explanation of why he must return Ian was told to: *"Come back in two days' time".* For the third time Ian set the room with his assistant. This time Maxwell did arrive but was only available for about five minutes (less in fact). Quickly handed a camera by his assistant, Ian managed six frames before Maxwell left the room, but the camera sounded odd. Ian realised the camera had no film. With a deadline to meet, he (and assistant) spent a frantic time racing up and down Fleet Street trying to buy a suitable picture of Maxwell. Considering the lack of regard Maxwell was held in at that time, this proved to be a very difficult task.

That incident was the exception. So much so that he was called upon time and again, usually at a moment's notice, to arrange to meet and then to photograph a raft of various news-worthy people.

With such a long list of celebrities who have sat or stood or even walked before Ian's lens there is not enough space here to detail every shoot. As well as those mentioned above, the following examples, hopefully, will show the extent and variety of those he photographed.

London, England

Francis Bacon (Born 28 October 1909, died 28 April 1992) was an Irish-born British painter. Since his death his reputation has grown steadily helped by a number of major works, assumed destroyed, emerging to set record prices at auction

In 1968, Ian went to photograph the writer Lawrence Durrell at his French home in the Provence Alpes. Travelling with a writer, Ian (and said writer, the identity of whom I have never been told) arrived at the author's front door. With his customary professionalism, Ian was ready to start work. His aim, as usual, was to make sure the portraits of Durrell showed the writer to best advantage. Having a background in journalism, Durrell was aware of how he wished his image to be portrayed. In this case informality was to be preferred. The way Ian worked would mean that the informal images would be all the more telling.

However, there was a problem. The writer who had been assigned to interview Durrell had a fondness for brandy. After a breakfast of a liquid kind, the journalist stopped twice more for brandy. After the initial introductions Durrell recognised the journalist was sloshed and put him in a spare room to sleep it off.

Initially mortified, Ian's embarrassment was quickly assuaged by Durrell's gentlemanly behaviour and informal approach to the session. There followed a day's photography where Ian was able to capture Durrell relaxing in his garden, sitting in an easy chair smoking a cigarette, drinking wine whilst engaged in animated conversation, drinking soup directly from a bowl and sharing a meal. The results speak for themselves, and offer an insight into the life of an affable man of letters who had a zest for living.

With the photography done it was time to go. Durrell had proved to be amiable company *"He was a great guy and I had a good shoot."* Ian recalls. However, the journalist was still asleep. *"Let's wake the bugger up!"* said Durrell who then poured black coffee into the man.

On the plane, the now-nearly sober writer quizzed Ian about the photographer's day. Later, when the copy was ready to go to press, Ian was surprised to read an article that was so well-written that there was no clue as to the inebriation of the author and his absence through an alcoholic haze.

There were shoots which proved more difficult to complete. These were usually the result of other people accompanying Ian and insisting upon taking over. Ian is not one to look kindly upon anyone accompanying him. I know, I've asked to be with him, but his stock response is *"No."* And he means it.

One difficult photoshoot that exemplifies this problem of being accompanied took place in 1964. Ian was sent to Number 10 Downing Street to photograph the then British Prime Minister, Harold Wilson. This was for the *Observer*. Wilson, for all his bluff Yorkshireman act, was media savvy and very protective of his public image.

He had enhanced this being a no-nonsense Yorkshireman by constantly smoking a pipe, eating his meals with dollops of HP sauce and wearing a Gannex coat. (This was a hardy, rainproof textile invented in 1951 by Kagan Textiles at the Elland Mill in West Yorkshire). All these eccentricities were part of Wilson's persona, assumed or not. The Prime Minister also took the unusual step of appearing on the very popular *Morecambe and Wise Show*, providing him with a potential audience of several millions.

For Ian, the problem with this session was more the sycophantic interference of the writer sent by the *Observer* than anything Wilson did. This eager writer and his need to constantly give directions made it impossible for Ian to achieve his customary, perceptive and trademark set of (relaxed) pictures. Whenever Wilson struck a pose, the writer would tell the Prime Minister how marvellous it was, at which point Wilson would remain so still he might well have been a waxwork model. Looking at the resultant images they show the Prime Minister standing stiffly by a long case clock in Downing Street, pipe in hand and, in another photograph, he sits in an easy chair sifting through papers. There is always the inevitable pipe clenched between his teeth whilst the man exudes a sense of barely concealed impatience.

Compare those Downing Street photographs with a set Ian made the following year when he had access to Anthony Crosland, then Minister of Education in Wilson's Government. The differences are very marked. Without an interfering writer to control the relationship between Ian and Crosland, Ian was free to follow

London, England
Alan Bennett at home. Bennett, with Jonathan Miller, Dudley Moore and Peter Cook, was an original member of the satirical show 'Beyond the Fringe' that transferred successfully to New York

his photographic inclinations. The results of that shoot show Crosland as a relaxed and friendly individual. Photographed at home rather than in an office, or any other formal situation, the politician comes across as amiable, a man who has left his ministerial face at the door or locked away in his red box. It works well even though, or perhaps because of, an absence of an image consultant hovering close by. With his cat, his wife (the American journalist Susan Catling), and his ready smile, we are left with an impression of an intelligent man, comfortable with this intrusion and confident enough to allow Ian the freedom to do what he does best.

At about the same time as the shots of Wilson and Crosland, Ian undertook a third story shoot, this time one that focused upon Wilson's then Chancellor of the Exchequer, Roy Jenkins. Though not as formal as those of Wilson, they were also very different to the images from the Crosland shoot. Jenkins is photographed behind his desk at the Treasury, working on a stack of papers and offering this carefully constructed "dedicated man of money" to the camera.

Another politician, but of a different persuasion, photographed by Ian was Margaret Thatcher. Back in 1979, Margaret Thatcher as Prime Minister was a hot topic. Being the first female British Prime Minister, this was a story worthy of international coverage. In a way, similar to Harold Wilson, Thatcher was another politician keen to maintain control over her public face. In an environmental portrait, Ian shows the "Iron Lady" dressed in a beige suit and wearing a headscarf because of the weather, surrounded by women in blue rainwear who are all also wearing headscarves. At that time, the headscarf was a female item of clothing full of social meaning. Worn across social class, from the Queen to factory workers, it also helped identify which generation you were from.

Working for *Newsweek*, Ian was on the election bus and shot the magazine's cover image of Mrs Thatcher on a doorstep with bags of shopping, the epitome of a thrifty housewife. In another photograph, Ian manages to capture a key moment in a public address when she highlights a point with her outstretched fingers. Her husband, Dennis, can be seen at the edge of the frame smiling, proud and paternal.

There are times when external events impinge upon the shoot. In 1966, Ian was in Italy to photograph the sculptor Henry Moore as he chose marble from the quarries at Caravaggio. The problem with the shoot was that Moore was an avid football fan and this was the year Britain hosted the World Cup. The stakes were high and, as it turned out, England went on to win the cup. Trying to complete his assignment, Ian was continually competing against the televising of the matches. The resultant pictures do reveal something of Moore the sculptor, though there are plenty of him watching the television. These Henry Moore images are also more examples of Ian's colour work.

Asking Ian to suggest which of his sessions was ideal, the one he chose was of the newspaper editor Sir Harold Evans. At the time, 1978, Evans was editing the British newspaper *The Sunday Times.*

"Why was this a good shoot?" Ian's answer to that question is simple, Evans ignored him. Ian was free to wander around the newsroom while Evans got on with his work.

There was no one to interfere with Ian as he went about his business. Indeed, the photographs of Evans feature him constantly working to make sure the newspaper is ready in time. He is either on this own studying layouts and copy or interacting with other *Sunday Times* employees. Those newsroom/print room photographs reveal a collegiate working environment though the status of Evans as the boss is never in doubt. As for the others in the newsroom, they play their part by ignoring Ian and are similarly absorbed in their work.

There were, sometimes, assignments which left Ian nonplussed. This was usually the result of how the subjects of the story behaved. Offering an example from 1968, Ian tells of travelling north to photograph the singer Dusty Springfield, who was then touring the region. Ian's photographs feature her performing and at rest. Springfield had a slender figure but a larger-than-life voice and a hair style to match. Catching the essence of the singer as she typically gave everything in one of her passionate renditions, those images are a counterpoint to the ones Ian took after the performance. There she is relaxing in her dressing room, "thank you" mail scattered around on the floor. Believing his work was done, it came as a surprise when he was woken up at 4am in the morning in his hotel by Dusty Springfield's assistant presenting him with a bouquet of flowers.

Ian has photographed many famous people favouring to place them in an environment they are familiar with. Ian's approach is to allow their personality to blossom so we can learn more about them. Ian is not really a head and shoulders sort of a portraitist. His series of colour images of Lord Yehudi Menuhin made in England and, later, at his Swiss home in Gstaad are exemplars of the Berry style. The shapes and tones Ian captures, the gentleness of the situations and the inclusion of others in the frame, especially when Menuhin is photographed interacting with others from the congregation after a concert in a Swiss church, all go to provide a very telling portrait of this much-loved musician.

Other musicians photographed by Ian were Menuhin's fellow violinist Igor Oistrakh and the New Zealand opera singer Kiri te Kanawa (whom Ian photographed in colour for a story in 1982). He has fond memories of photographing Dame Kiri, and the results testify to the relaxed and productive session. Dame Kiri, an avid golfer, was happy to go along with any and all ideas, and happy to accompany Ian to a golf course.

Other stories Ian remembers with affection are usually the result of the amiable and co-operative nature of the subjects. Two in this vein were the authors Muriel Spark and Penelope Mortimer, both tellingly photographed on black and white film. The results of those shoots reveal a playful side to be a characteristic shared by the two authors.

Perhaps, the stories that spanned the gap between formal and informal were those where the subject was restricted by how far they could participate. One such was Professor Stephen Hawking. The steady deterioration of Professor Hawking became a limiting factor in how the various sessions with Ian would play out.

Cambridge, England

Professor Stephen Hawking (8 January 1942 – 14 March 2018) was an English theoretical physicist, cosmologist, author and director of research at the Centre for Theoretical Cosmology at the University of Cambridge. Between 1979 and 2009, he was the Lucasian Professor of Mathematics at Cambridge, widely viewed as one of the most prestigious academic posts in the world. He is perhaps most widely known for his book 'A Brief History of Time'

When Ian visited his home in Cambridge in 1977, he was able to photograph the professor laughing at the antics of his then wife Jane and their two children as they tended a barbecue in the back garden. In other photographs taken at the same session Professor Hawking gives his son and daughter a ride on his mobility chair. Still in the garden, the mood is gentle and the professor is photographed in profile while Lucy, his daughter, swings to and fro on a swing fixed to the branch of a mature tree. Later, inside, Professor Hawking is caught in the soft light coming in from the window as he listens to his wife playing the piano.

"He was a really good guy. I liked him a lot. He was good to be with." This feeling of respect was reciprocated to the point where Professor Hawking asked Ian to be his photographer. For Ian, though it was an attractive and flattering honour, it was not possible. Ian's peripatetic life meant such commitments were impractical. Still, Ian returned several times to photograph the professor in Cambridge.

Trying to capture the essential humanity of Hawking, Ian concentrated upon photographing him in situations where he was relaxed and interacting with people he knew well and felt comfortable with. One place where this was possible was in his Cambridge University office with his long-time secretary.

For one of those assignments Ian photographed Professor Hawking in front of the life-sized marble statue of Sir Isaac Newton. Symbolic though the photographs might be, Ian feels they failed. "The lighting was very bad and I had to set up a whole battery of lights."

On another visit, Ian accompanied Professor Hawking around the grounds of Cambridge University. From a photographic point of view the problem was that it rained, hard. The professor is photographed swathed in a dark coat to protect him from the weather, a head emerging from the sheltering cloth. "I never wanted to focus on his face. I felt that was wrong". Having said this, amongst the photographs there is one in particular that brings the viewer close to Stephen Hawking's face. It is a monochrome image that concentrates upon the professor's head and shoulders. There is another, a similar one that is in colour, but it is the monochrome image that illustrates the true nature of the man. There is something gentle about his look as he dominates the frame. It is a face full of thoughts, an attractive face that looks younger than his 44 years. If anything, it is boyish. Without the paraphernalia of the wheelchair and the communications gadgets, you are left with just the man and his greatness.

One commission that Ian talks fondly of was his portrait session with the Irish Poet Seamus Heaney. Ian took Heaney to a pub-cum-village store, typical of the region where Heaney lived. This allowed both men to share the craic along with a drink, and then for Ian to produce some relaxed and intimate shots of Heaney. With Heaney complicit, Ian photographed him at home with his wife and children. What you see in these photographs is a very human man surrounded by love and grounded in family life; in many ways the essence of Heaney's poetry. There is one more venue where Ian and Heaney go and there the poet rests on the parapet of a bridge, overlooking a slow-moving river. It wouldn't take too big a leap of the imagination to see the scene as being where the young Heaney came to gather his frogspawn celebrated in his 1966 poem, *Death of a Naturalist*.

The quintessential American female conflict journalist, and one-time wife of Ernest Hemingway, Martha Gellhorn, came to London and Ian was there to photographer her. Gellhorn had married Hemingway in 1940, after travelling with him and reporting on the Spanish Civil War. Their marriage had not lasted and they divorced in 1945. Gellhorn was noted for her reports from the war-torn regions of Europe, continuing to do so during the Vietnam War and the Arab-Israeli conflicts of the 1960s and 1970s. She was a legend amongst journalists, especially those who ventured into conflict zones. One of Magnum Photo's founders, Robert Capa, had visited Hemingway and Gellhorn in 1940-41 in Sun Valley Idaho. Once again, in 1953, when Capa was in Italy, he had photographed Gellhorn amidst the ruins of Paestum. Twenty-four years later Gellhorn was in London, being photographed by another of Magnum's members. This time it was Ian Berry who recorded the smile and vivacity of this legend.

Aberfan October 21st 1966

When the slag heap of mud and pit rubbish slid over the Pantglas Junior School in Aberfan it became one of those benchmark events, along with the assassination of President Kennedy and the attack on the Twin Towers in New York, by which we can plot the passing of time. Aberfan is all we need to say to recall the moment we first heard the news, such was the power of the incident. Though for Ian it was just one terrible situation amongst so many. Managing to separate himself from the horror, he looks at the photographs and selects a couple of images he feels meet his exacting standards sufficient to make them satisfactory.

I remember exactly where I was when the BBC announced the disaster on their *6 O'clock News*. I was standing in the lounge of one of the University of London's halls of residence, in Russell Square. The television was on and those of us standing there were concentrating upon the flickering screen avid for more news. As the truth began to sink in there was a long and palpable silence.

The Coal Board was responsible for the safe disposal of pit waste but the Aberfan slag heap was sited higher up the hillside, above the school, and its stability had been compromised by heavy rains. It didn't take much for the slag heap to slither like some malevolent lava flow down the hill and cover the school.

116 children and 28 adults died and, as a nation, we shared in that sadness. We witnessed the frantic work efforts of the miners and the volunteers as they fought the slurry. Our understanding of the tragedy and the feeling of shared horror is due, to a great extent, to the images captured by Ian and the other photographers at the scene.

Ian Berry arrived in Aberfan as darkness fell. Such was the urgent need to rescue as many as possible that even darkness did not prevent the teams from digging and clearing away the debris. The few who had survived were already free. What now determined the frantic activity was a search for bodies. By then any other feelings were more of hope than expectation. The dead were slowly being released from the clinging hold of the muck. Ant-like, men from Aberfan and surrounding pits were frantically searching, many for members of their own families. Wearing their pit gear, their colliers' helmets still on their heads, stripped down to their coal-stained vests, these fathers and brothers, friends and neighbours worked throughout the night. Ian photographed the Dante's Inferno-like scenes as smoke rose from the still-hot slag heap, made all the more surreal by the floodlights that back-lit these frantic efforts.

For a while this community, torn apart by the loss of so many children, was united by their single need to dig.

Like some reticulated serpent, bucket-chains were formed as the slurry was passed back to be dumped and the empty bucket returned along the chain to the head of the line. Bucket after bucket moved back and forth, in a ceaseless effort to save what could be saved. Ian captured the minutiae of the rescue efforts.

In the grey light of dawn, members of the Salvation Army carried round trays of sandwiches for the exhausted workers. Down in the village, women were making endless cups of tea. The scene was *"...typically British, with everyone helping out and going about the job of recovering the bodies quietly and with thoroughness".* Ian explains.

With daylight illuminating the scene, Ian could complete the telling of the story. Close behind the Salvation Army came the older, secondary school lads standing, at first, transfixed by the damage, then spurred into action as they started to do what they could to help, but not before Ian had photographed them and the universal look of disbelief on their faces. It was the faces, the little details of devastation, that would tell the real story. Those lads had recently been pupils at the primary school.

"It was chaos everywhere. You were trying to keep out of the way because it was pretty emotional; if you were there with a camera it meant that you weren't contributing to the rescue...

"It was just a case of doing what one could, climbing around in the mud. It was pretty messy and I was trying not to get in the way of people working on recovery." Ian Berry

I asked Ian if there was any resentment from the workers whilst he was there? He said not. Later, talking with Ian's friend and fellow photographer, Patrick Ward, about Ian's ability to become invisible and to be sympathetic to his subjects, it came as no surprise to Patrick that Ian's presence had been accepted. *"They had probably not even noticed him there."* Looking at Ian's photographs they all have a narrative thread, typical of a photographer used to telling a story. He stood back and gave each image the space it needed.

Throughout his photographic life, people have found that Ian's mild manner makes him easy to accept, and you feel it is in his nature to be suitably respectful towards his subjects. His friend and fellow photographer, Tom Stoddart, called him a "Gentle Hunter". Robert Capa, one of Magnum's founders, is noted for saying the photographer should like the people they are photographing and show them that they are liked. Couple this with an eye for detail and a firm grasp of what is happening and how it should be best photographed and you have the guiding principles behind Ian's work. However, with the camera to his eye, little else exists but the task in hand. He is so firmly focused upon photographing that he is editing his work even before he presses the shutter.

"Try and get it right in the camera first." Ian Berry

Being an experienced Magnum photographer, Ian was well-versed in the realities of photographing complex and emotionally challenging situations. From its founding in 1947, the Magnum Photo Agency has sought to remain true to the traditions of humane and compassionate photography. It was not just a process of obtaining images that would sell, more of a desire to convey the truth of an event or place. Ian's priority has always been to report what he saw as honestly as possible.

The Aberfan aftermath

It was obvious that Aberfan was an event of enormous importance and Ian felt that his task was to record what he saw and to show the suffering and the heroism of this Welsh mining community to the rest of the world. As later events unfolded both Ian's photographs, and those of fellow Magnum photographer David Hurn, became crucial in resolving the matter of compensation, as well as challenging the attitude of the National Coal Board. At the time of the disaster the attitude of senior NCB managers was hard to understand. It lacked any semblance of compassion or understanding.

Lord Robens, the then chairman of the National Coal Board avoided visiting Aberfan immediately, preferring instead to attend a ceremony installing him as Chancellor of the University of Surrey.

As if to add insult to injury, details emerged that the management's offers of compensation were risible. It was to counter the offer along with the attitude of the NCB that the photographs of the event were most useful. The NCB's belittling of the event was insulting, and compounded by offering only £50 in compensation for each child. Lord Robens justified this paltry sum by saying it would be irresponsible to offer these working class parents too much money as they would be *"corrupted by such riches".* The £50 was later upped to £500, which was still deemed, by the NCB at the time, to be exorbitant. David Hurn said, in 2018, that he felt that: *"Ian and I, we did a good deed that day."*

Spending a couple of days there, Ian was able to photograph the visit by Prince Philip, Duke of Edinburgh, who came to offer what sympathy he could. This was on Saturday 22nd October. After this, Ian had to leave and was not there when nine days later Her Majesty Queen Elizabeth and Prince Philip came to express their sympathy, an act that was much admired by the villagers who felt that the Queen and Prince Philip were genuine in their sympathy, and not tainted by politics.

Attending Cardiff University recently, Ian returned to Aberfan to photograph the village as it is now, with the pits closed, the old school demolished and a new school built on a different, a safer, site. Standing next to the memorial, in the Welsh rain, he finally completed his Aberfan story with a photograph of the Memorial Garden.

Aberfan, Glamorgan, Wales

Exhausted police, miners and helpers are silhouetted against the temporary arc lights and against the steam coming off the coal mine slurry after digging all day for survivors of the disaster

Aberfan, Glamorgan, Wales
Exhausted miners and workers, who have been digging for hours, are offered food by a member of the Salvation Army

Canada

In 1967, Ian went to Canada on a story for *The Observer*. This was to be a lengthy assignment and Ian had been given a writer who was to stay with him for a week or so. The plan was to drive across Canada starting from the West Coast. Prior to the long-distance drive, Ian wished to go to Newfoundland Island to illustrate a story on winter. This was to cover the fishing industry and the lives of those living in this extreme part of Canada. Ian also wanted to go to Churchill in Hudson's Bay, Manitoba, to photograph the Hudson's Bay Company, again in winter.

Never one to expect five-star accommodation, Ian would spend his evenings wherever the locals were to be found. This was invariably a way of obtaining background shots and local colour, along with a wealth of information along and making himself known to those he might be photographing later.

On a bitterly cold evening in Churchill, Ian was in the local pub. Outside, the wind-blown snow was deep as even more fell. Inside, it was warm and convivial.

Through the bar's door came a First Nation youth, eager to leave the arctic conditions outside. He wanted a drink. The relationship of First Nation and white Canadians can be fraught at times. Recently, the First Nations have developed a greater political awareness and have become more assertive, back then it was a different story. Trouble is often the result of alcohol and drug abuse, but in the 1960s the First Nation peoples were less aware of their place in Canadian society. Though consumption of any booze is not something that is encouraged, even amongst the white population, its effects amongst the First Nation peoples can be devastating. In this case, the young lad had a couple of drinks and was then told he'd had enough and should leave. With his departure, the evening in the bar continued as before.

The consequences of asking this youth to leave became all too clear in the morning when his body was discovered a few yards from the bar entrance, frozen to death in the snow. Saddened by the tragedy, Ian decided to remain there a little longer and spend time with the boy's family. His presence was obviously welcomed as, apart from his parents, Ian was the only other person at the funeral. There is a sad photograph Ian made, taken from one side of the coffin which was a crude affair with a simple painted cross on the lid and a plaque placed above it. The picture is of the boy's mother, wrapped up against the cold, looking down with the universal sadness any and every mother feels when forced to bury her child. *The Observer* ran Ian's story on Canada's Centennial and included one picture of the funeral.

The Joys of being with a writer

Writers can, at times, create problems for a photographer. Each has his or her own expectations and differing ways of approaching an assignment. At times it can become a tussle for which one takes the lead. Having suffered the interference from a writer at a Number 10 Downing Street shoot (the Harold Wilson story) it was on the Canadian Confederation Celebrations story where Ian suffered further irritation. This time, he was partnered with a novice writer who thought of herself as being the most important part of the team.

After obtaining their accreditation in Ottawa, the two of them travelled on to Vancouver to start the journey. This was to be a west to east trip across the vast expanse of over 3,000 miles that is the "belly" of the nation. The Trans-Canada Highway is often a straight road that lavishly warns drivers of a bend well before you arrive at it. In parts of the country, you can drive for miles before encountering habitation. This could hardly be conducive to team building when one of the team regarded Ian as being there merely to illustrate her words. This meant that at every first meeting she would introduce Ian as *"my photographer"*.

With admirable patience (and his sense of humour kept intact), Ian bided his time until he had a chance to introduce her, on one occasion, as his caption writer. This was not well received.

Early in their journey, they arrived in the Province of Alberta and the large city of Calgary, famous for the Calgary Stampede. During Stampede, Calgary loses all its inhibitions when everything and everyone goes "cowboy". Granted, Calgary is a very successful oil town and has few inhibitions anyway, but come Stampede white hats and cowboy boot are *de rigeur*. This is the place where any aspiring wild-cow milker worth his salt comes to try their luck. It is a town full of chuck wagons and riders with more broken bones than any sensible person would wish to admit to. Amongst the many bizarre pursuits this is the one venue where biting a wild horse's ear makes sense. In this case it is necessary for one rider to jump off his own horse, grab the wild one round the neck then, as a distraction, bite the nearest available ear. At this point, others of the team then saddle the horse ready for yet another crew member to jump on and ride, hopefully.

The brief was for the writer to interview one of these fearless rodeo riders, whilst Ian would photograph him. The venue was out of Calgary, on one of the many ranches that surround the city. All went well until the writer proudly announced that she could ride. Whether it was her certainty or merely Canadian good manners, but a horse was provided and the writer duly mounted. The belief amongst most Canadian riders is that, if you can ride an English saddle then an American saddle is a "piece of cake". Whatever she did to encourage the horse is unknown, but it took off at a gallop. The hectic progress of the two took them in a wide circle around the paddock.

Whilst the writer hung onto the horse it chose to go behind the barn, one of those large, red painted wooden structures so typical of this part of Canada. Out of sight for a brief while, it was something of a surprise to Ian and the Canadian when only the horse emerged moments later. There was no sign of the writer. For whatever reason, and that was never disclosed, she had fallen off. What the Canadian rodeo rider thought Ian, diplomatically, won't tell me but the horse seemed pleased, and being a well-mannered Canadian horse it obviously thought it best to do the deed out of sight and so save the girl's blushes.

Sometimes you are fortunate and work with a good writer

Other writers could be a joy. In 1988, Ian was asked by the *National Geographic* book division to work on their project to photograph some of the Great Parks around the world. It was suggested that Ian would visit two: the Lake District National Park in the North of England and the Fjordland National Park on the South Island of New Zealand. Walking the four-day Milford Trail, Routeburn and Greenstone tracks, Ian tramped them twice, once alone and then with the writer Paul Theroux.

India

Like his relationship with Africa, Ian is called back time and again to India. It was here that he spent time with the Indian-based writer William Dalrymple. Whether out of a sense of mischief or because it was a genuine suggestion, Dalrymple advised Ian to visit a particular temple where there was an elephant who participated in the daily worship. Not sure what role the elephant played, the potential was too intriguing to ignore.

Keen to photograph the temple and its activities anyway, Ian duly arrived and witnessed the flagellation of some of the congregation, as they were tied to a tree in the temple compound. The elephant was there but it was *"not that much to write home about".* However, the real activity was inside the temple complex and so Ian entered. The trouble was, that to gain entry and participate in whatever way, you had to remove all your clothing. For the rest of the shoot Ian, naked as the day he was born, moved amongst the participants trying hard to retain his modesty with a carefully placed camera bag.

The initial intention was to visit Dalrymple to hear his stories but it had taken an age for Ian to find his home. Dalrymple lived in a part of Delhi where the streets had no names and the houses no numbers. The author was less than welcoming and Ian was left wondering if the suggestion to visit the temple was a way of getting rid of him.

It was in 1993, in Kolkata (then known as Calcutta), that Ian photographed the work of the street doctor Jack Preger OBE. Preger came from Manchester but spent a great deal of his working life in various parts of the world. After working in South and Central America he moved to the newly independent Bangladesh. He worked in the various refugee camps, setting up a 90 bed clinic in Dhaka. Having exposed a child-smuggling racket despite government warnings not to, he was deported and crossed the border into India.

In India, he initially worked for Mother Teresa's charity until he decided to set up his own clinic, Calcutta Rescue. Even here, on the streets of Calcutta, his work was far from trouble-free. It became necessary to employ local doctors to circumvent government restrictions. Ian's photographs show the tarpaulin-covered street clinic he constructed on a daily basis, along with the many poor people who frequented them. Many of these patients were lepers, some in an advanced state.

Close to being deported yet again, Preger took the Foreigners' Registration Office of West Bengal to court when they charged him with being an unregistered missionary after an American missionary organisation sent him funds.

In South India, with his wife Kathie, Ian spent time at the Ashram of Dom Bede Griffiths (1906 to 1993). Dom Bede was one of the leading thinkers who worked to bring a closer understanding between Christianity and Hinduism. Ian and Kathie stayed at the Ashram when Dom Bede was very ill, and in extremis. This was 1993. There is a typically non-intrusive picture made by Ian showing the ailing Dom Bede, thin and lying on his cot, talking with a fellow priest. The sensitive nature of this photograph reflects both the compassion of the photographer and the asceticism of the subject.

One of the problems Ian faced whilst at the ashram was that of eating with his fingers. Under normal circumstances, eating curry and rice would not be a problem but when your job means you take photographs, the last thing you want is to have messy fingers. Seeing his dilemma, one of his fellow diners provided Ian with a spoon. Unable to return the spoon, I believe Ian may still possess it.

Back in Kolkata (in 2009) Ian was photographing a story about water. Here there were standpipes in the street to be turned on twice a day. Being a predominantly Hindu nation where the cow is held to be sacred, it came as no surprise when, as he prepared to photograph people gathered around a standpipe, Ian witnessed a cow taking precedence, making its stately way through the crowd and having a drink. Ian has a photograph he likes that shows the imperious nature of the cow, and its ability to know there is no reason for it to queue. Not taking its turn is something Indian cows do.

An itinerant life

Ian's stories, those which he continues to work on, still provide him with a life less ordinary. Perhaps it is this feeling of never knowing what may come next that advises the life of a photojournalist. Travel is one thing, but having the discomfort of the journey ameliorated by resting in a cosy hotels does not fit with Ian's experiences. A tin shack in the middle of nowhere, one that is running alive with bugs and the constant presence of overly inquisitive strangers is more likely to be his experience. Planning for the worst and expecting the worst offers the potential pleasure of a surprise ending.

Ian's life being one of never being sure what may come next, provides him with a richness and a variety denied to many others, even amongst the photographic community. Whether it is an overseas assignment or something more domestic it becomes the photographer to be more a boy scout, one that is always prepared. There are times when the overseas stories come in a relentless stream and the visa stamps fill the passport. I made a quick tally of the countries Ian has visited and lost count when I reached 130, but my counting did not take into consideration the number of return visits, or those countries where access was obtained without official recognition. Over his working life Ian could be photographing in Cyprus one day and then flying off to Dusseldorf the next. Watching Ian interacting with others you come to realise his approach is invariably the same, regardless. There is definite air of calm and an absence of confrontation. His charm and naturally gentle approach invariably wins over his subject. How else could he beguile the Avon Ladies of Canton?

Simla, India
This religious procession takes place every winter, often in a heavy snowfall

Africa once more

To look back over the stories he has covered you see there is a certain part of the world where he has spent a great deal of his working life. This is Africa. It is a continent to which he is drawn time and again. From those early years of his photographic life till now, it has been the venue for many of his most impressive stories. Being a continent of many faces and conditions, it offers ever-changing (and challenging) opportunities, and Ian has covered just about all of them.

From his early years working on domestic stories for *Drum* to his recent work for *Fair Trade* documenting the gold miners of Uganda, Ian has done it all. There are obvious highlights along with the "bread and butter" work. One such was his monumental 1970 trip through Africa from North to South before he travelled home through India, Afghanistan and points west to make it back to London. After working on a Christian Aid assignment on the impact of global food production in Ghana, Ian heard of the practice of families selling their children to fishermen. This piqued Ian's interest and his subsequent photographs resulted in a book called *Sold into Slavery* (CDPEDITIONS, France, August 2008).

A travelling exhibition illustrating the book *Disposable People* used work by the Magnum photographers Abbas, Ian Berry, Stuart Franklin, Jim Goldberg, Susan Meiselas, Paolo Pelegrín, Chris Steele-Perkins and Alex Webb.

It was supported by Arts Council England, MTV Europe Foundation, Christian Aid and Concern World Wide. The exhibition and subsequent book included work by fellow Magnum photographers: Abbas, Stuart Franklin, Jim Goldberg, Susan Meiselas, Paolo Pelegrín, Chris Steele-Perkins and Alex Webb. There is no doubt that Ian has left his mark upon the photographic record of the continent. Like his portfolio of China, there is a sizeable archive of African photographs to cover just about every aspect of the continent's changing story over the past 60 dynamic years.

The travelling continues. Ian spent time in Columbia early in 2018 and then Sicily in late spring. Driving his camper van around Europe or hiring cars, Ian is constantly on the go. A recent trip to Spain saw him negotiating steep mountain roads in the Pyrenees when the brakes on his van failed. But, typical of the man, he modestly says it was just *"one of those things,"* not something worth fussing over.

Attempting to catalogue the countries that Ian has visited and photographed, it would be easier to list those he hasn't visited. During one of our conversations this subject was raised, and Ian said there were two countries he wished to visit: Iceland and Cuba (the latter before the old cars and the 1950s atmosphere disappear).

Considering the varied nature of Ian's stories, you may come to the conclusion that the range of subjects, whilst eclectic, means he does not have a genre, is not easily pigeon-holed. Whilst some photographers can be be regarded by the public and themselves as art photographers and others see themselves as specialising in conflict, Ian is there to explore the human experience.

Transvaal (Gauteng), South Africa

Miners underground in a Transvaal gold mine where the only light comes from the lamps on their helmets

Consider the broad theme of gold mining in Africa. Ostensibly, a subject easily covered, but the subtleties that lie behind the extraction of gold in terms of social and tribal pressures make this a nuanced story. There is a photographic trail starting with Ian's early work in 1961, a time when he photographed the Transvaal mines. This trail becomes a story of greed and hard labour. Returning to the region in 1962, he covered mining in Witwatersrand. In 1968, he was in the Reef region near Johannesburg photographing gold mining once more.

Then, in 2016, Ian was in Uganda, documenting the lives of the miners in the Torono region. The story was completed in conjunction with the Fair Trade organisation. As organisations such as the NGOs seek to make changes, working for charities like Fair Trade provide an increasingly popular way for photographers to work on assignments they find conducive.

From those early stories where the miners wore helmets and worked underground, where Ian was able to capture the claustrophobic atmospheric in his monochrome pictures, it comes as a shock when you consider the crude techniques evinced in his Uganda images. This was the theme of a story from 2016 when Ian was contracted to follow the gold seam that underscored three countries. Uganda was the only one of the three where no rules applied and health and safety was non-existentt. As a consequence, the lack of restrictions and regulations meant that the working conditions were primitive at best, and deadly at worst.

Looking at Ian's images from that story you are aware the villagers mined in a way similar, if not identical, to the way prospectors worked in the early days of the Klondike Gold Rush. Considering the age-old mining methods employed, Ian's monochrome photographs could have been made any time during the past 150 years. However, come to look at the colour pictures and your perceptions shift. The young men are wearing brightly-coloured, European football club shirts.

As for the dangers, it transpires that these open mines have a tendency to weaken the soil structure and, as a result, many of the houses where mining takes place collapse.

When the Baltic States became members of the European Union in 2002, the British Council asked Ian to travel there to photograph possible opportunities "to spread the word". Ian was to work with the assistance of the British ambassadors in the three countries. Of the three it was the ambassador in Lithuania who expressed the greatest interest and Ian is quite open when he admits the ambassador's commitment is reflected in the pictures. It helps when, working on such a story, officials who know the area and the requirements of the photographer co-operate and ease the processes.

Sometimes, a photographer can find the gods of the lens smiling, offering the equivalent of BOGOF (buy one get one free). In 1995, Ian went to work on a story for the German *Zeit Magazine*. This was to Kazakhstan. The freebee was to be a chance to photograph a visiting team from the BBC there, supposedly, to teach Kazakh television how to make daytime dramas. *"The Kazakh TV crews knew very well how to make the soaps. They didn't need the BBC at all."*

The early days of the 21st Century saw Ian return to one of his favourite cities: Berlin. This was to work on a story for *Stern Magazine*. Berlin is a city to wander around and photograph, and is very close to Ian's heart. It's a city where he can amble, free of many of the constraints placed upon him by a tight brief. In 2000, the wall had been down for a few years, long enough to allow for some sort of reconciliation of East and West, yet there were still traces of the differences, should you know where to look.

When Ian was in Berlin in 1963, he was there at the height of the Cold War and his winter landscape images were peopled with anonymous figures wrapped against the cold. The stark black and white pictures of figures were seen against the snow and the general feel was one of a dystopian post-war city where characters from a John Le Carré novel might be waiting in the shadow of a shop doorway, smoking a *Gitane*.

Fast forward to 2000 and, this time in colour, there are all the old places to revisit and photograph: the Tiergarten, the Kurfurstendamm, the Brandenburg Gate and the Reichstag. But these are all transformed. The menace has gone as have so many of the reminders of the Russian Occupation. In Ian's images, there are Korean dancers at the Brandenburg Gate where once the Russian Army had stood guard next to a static T34 tank. People are photographed dancing in the clubs especially those, such as the Trumpete Club and the Sage Club, where once you worried about being overheard saying something careless that might get you in trouble with the East German Police.

Where you once approached Checkpoint Charlie and knew you were at the sharp edge of the Cold War (where you were obliged to leave details of your trip to "The Other Side" with your own country's armed forces... just in case), there is now a gift shop.

An immigrant woman is photographed begging on the Kurfurstendamm when once it was the sight of old soldiers asleep in hedges and on benches rendered oblivious by whatever alcohol they could find. Aftershave and antifreeze were popular choices back then. In one photograph, an elderly lady hangs out of the small window of her apartment, around which are the remains of bullet holes. They make the wall look like a piece of Swiss cheese. The brick wall has even been painted a cheese yellow.

Across what was once the Wall is the Reichstag. Back in the 1960s it was virtually impossible to visit but now, with it being the seat of government for the unified Germany, it attracts tourists by the bus load. And Ian captures the vagaries of the visitors and their ice-cream enjoyment. What was once the object of the Red Army's final offensive is now just like so many other tourist attractions: one to tick off the list.

Should we wish to catalogue every one of Ian's overseas trips (and forget the assignments from nearer home) we would have to use several hundred pages, especially if we printed one image from each of those assignments.

With an average of 26 major assignments per year and 60 years of material to delve into, that works out to be something in the region of 1560 individual stories. You can see the limitations in trying to identify and report on each one. As his wife, Kathie, says it would be like trying to write *War and Peace*. As we said in the introduction, we'll let a well-chosen selection of Ian's pictures speak for themselves.

Back to the late 1960s

For some reason, the zeitgeist current at the time of the late 1960s was one of revolution and protest. In Britain it was manifest though musical expression and the anti-war protests in Grosvenor Square outside the American Embassy. Photographing this protest Ian exhibited his well-practised baton-avoiding skills. In the annals of British protest this was a major event and was met with a considerable police presence. His old friend from Africa, Jürgen Schadeberg, was also covering the demonstration. *"I saw Ian across from me, gracefully dodging the mounted police. He remained immune whilst I was hit several times."*

In France, Ian's fellow Magnum photographers were covering the students as they tore up the pavé from the Paris streets and used them to fight the police. Of the Magnum photographers who were there one was Henri Cartier-Bresson, photographed standing on a fallen tree by Marc Riboud. Ian was in Czechoslovakia. His story of rebellion and social upheaval would be shot in Prague. Ian Berry would be the sole Western photojournalist to enter Czechoslovakia on the day the Russians invaded.

The Prague Spring and the Russian Invasion

To understand the background of the "how" and the "why" of the Russian Invasion (and the Boy's Own story of how Ian Berry came to be the only western photojournalist to make his way to Prague during the opening days of the occupation), we need to consider the background that led to that heady summer of 1968.

Back in the 1960s the world was ideologically and politically divided between the West and the East. Militarily, the West had a co-operative alliance of nations made manifest in membership of the North Atlantic Treaty Organisation (NATO). Initially, it was an agreement for mutual support between France and Britain signed in March 1947. This agreement grew until, by 1949, it included the United States, Canada, Portugal, Italy, Norway, Denmark, Iceland and the Benelux countries. As NATO grew it was considered to be an existential threat to the Soviet Union and its satellites. As a counter-balance the Kremlin organised its military response: the Warsaw Pact.

The post-war period saw both sides develop and stockpile sufficient nuclear weapons to destroy all life on earth. With such an abundance of military equipment feeding the paranoia of the military of both blocks, expenditure spiralled out of control. Proxy wars became a common outlet for this tension and even a country as financially constrained as post-war Britain was committing 10% of its budget to defence spending. Today, Britain is spending a maximum of 2.4% at best. This constant race to ensure a parity between the two armed camps took the world ever closer to what was clinically/cynically labeled mutually assured destruction (MAD).

Perhaps the most blatant evocation of this tension became known as the Cuban Missile Crisis. In 1962, the Soviet Russians attempted to place ballistic missiles on the island of Cuba. This led to a standoff between the Russian ships as they sailed to Cuba loaded with missiles, and elements of the US Navy. In the end, it was Khrushchev who appeared to back down. What is probably less well known is that President Kennedy agreed to remove the missiles America had placed in Turkey, close to the Soviet Union's Southern border.

Only five years later, in 1967, the world once again held its breath. This time, events in Czechoslovakia were the cause for concern. The roots of the trouble dated back to the end of the First World War when Czechoslovakia was created out of the debris of the Austro-Hungarian Empire. A forced marriage between the Czech and Slovak peoples was far from amicable. Immediately prior to Second World War the Slovak state had been recognised as an autonomous country and became a client state of Germany. Slovak troops had already been absorbed into the the German Army and they were the only other Axis contingent to join the German forces when they invaded Poland in 1939.

The end of the Second World War saw a brief flowering of a moderate, independent Czechoslovakia. That is until the Czech Communist Party engineered control of the government. Stalin's policy towards the West meant that Czechoslovakia was an essential section of his "Iron Curtain". In this way Czechoslovakia became a Warsaw Pact country, a satellite providing additional troops and a physical barrier between the motherland of Russia and the capitalist West.

Regrettably, The Kremlin's policy of central control was predicated upon the needs of poorer, agrarian-dominated countries like East Germany, Hungary and Poland. Stalin failed to take into consideration the sophisticated industrial economy of Czechoslovakia. In 1919, Czechoslovakia had been blessed, or cursed, with over 70% of the Austro-Hungarian Empire's industrial capacity.

Prague, Czechoslovakia
Czechs listen to news of the Russian invasion on a portable radio

Prague, Czechoslovakia
A group of young Czechs harangue Russian soldiers who have invaded their city

Prague, Czechoslovakia
Russian tanks are positioned across the street to prevent any vehicular access

Prague, Czechoslovakia
A Russian soldier chases a Czech man in Wenceslas Square

This economic mismatch apart, the fraternal visit of Marshall Tito of Yugoslavia to Prague was a blatant slap in the face for the Soviet hierarchy. Never one to conform to what Moscow believed was the essential party line. Tito was a continual thorn in the side of the Kremlin hardliners. He was seen as being too independently minded and friendly to the West (and therefore uncontrollable, and unreliable).

The younger members of the Czechoslovak Communist Party wanted to develop a style of communism akin to that of Yugoslavia, with its fewer restrictions and a more liberal relationship with the rest of the world. To keep faith with his communist elders the leader of these young turks, Alexander Dubcek, explained this not to be seen as a move towards liberalism, but the development of Democratic Communism. It was, said Dubcek, *"Communism with a Human Face".*

Kowtowing to the Kremlin was not a part of the Czech personality. When it became clear what the shape and intent of this Democratic Communism was, it drew universal support from the Czech people.

1968 was a restless year. Across the world, the Baby Boomers born after the end of Second World War had come of age. In Paris, in Poland, in the US and the UK there was general unrest. Faced with the situation in Prague, Leonid Brezhnev, the General Secretary of the Central Committee of the Communist Party, visited Prague to witness for himself the growing antipathy towards the established, hardline Communist leadership. Repression was obviously not working. It must have been clear to Brezhnev that the established order was beyond saving. When the Stalinist President, Antonin Novotny, fell from power in January 1968, his fate was accepted by the Kremlin. What was there to worry about? Alexander Dubcek, Novotny's replacement, was a close ally of the Soviet Union, wasn't he?

Appearances can be deceptive. Until Dubcek felt the time was right he played a canny game. The slow, imperceptible, loosening of state control in Czechoslovakia (one that allowed foreign travel, limited the power of the secret police and permitted a market economy to flourish) eventually reached a point where it became obvious even to the Kremlin hierarchy that Dubcek was, in fact, not their man. The reforms were going too far. The fear was that, if this liberalisation was to continue, the country would become uncontrollable. That would lead to a breach in the "Wall".

March 1968 had seen the spread of student protests, starting in Poland. After Novotny's resignation the accumulation of events both behind the Iron Curtain and in the West, led Yuri Andropov, the Chairman of the KGB, to issue a statement likening conditions in Czechoslovakia to the situation that pertained in Hungary in 1956. He spoke of an *"outward appearance of chaos"* which Andropov believed would finally lead to the rise of a social democracy. Any compromising of Russia's security could not be tolerated. Maintaining the integrity of Czechoslovakia, and its border with West Germany and Austria, was essential.

In a Pravda article of 26th September 1968 Sergei Kovalev outlined the doctrine that later became the cornerstone of Soviet Foreign Policy, The Brezhnev Doctrine. In a speech on November 13th 1968, the chief architect of the policy, Leonid Brezhnev himself, stated *"When forces that are hostile to socialism try to turn the development of some socialist country towards capitalism, it becomes not only a problem for the country concerned, but a common problem and concern of all socialist countries."*

In April 1968 the Dubcek Government announced a plan to remove State Control from industry and allowed freedom of speech along with a multiplicity of alternative political parties. From this moment on, a Russian-led invasion became inevitable.

In the West, those charged with making policy had memories of the recent Cuban Missile Crisis and the 1956 Hungarian Uprising advising their proposed plan of action. As for the Western media, they were *"Like greyhounds in the slips, straining upon the start".* (Henry V, Shakespeare) and journalists of all persuasions were sniffing the wind and making ready. With their bags packed they waited for a call from their editors. Those editors, sensing a major story, began to plan accordingly.

The Magnum photographer Eric Lessing, had covered the Hungarian uprising of 1956 and produced a detailed, and definitive, illustrated account. That uprising had cost an estimated 2,500 to 3,000 Hungarian lives with a further 13,000 wounded, though the Soviet forces would never confirm this. 722 Soviet troops died and 1,540 were wounded.

Following the crushing of the uprising, there had been a Hungarian diaspora. Was that to be repeated? Would the toll be even higher this time?

As the world waited, in London Ian Berry procured an appropriate travel visa, made sure he had packed sufficient rolls of 35mm film and was ready go.

The expected telephone call came early on the morning of 20th August. At 6:00am, Magnum's Paris Bureau Chief [Russ Melcher] rang Ian asking him if he was interested in going to Prague; *"The Russians have invaded! Don [McCullin] has already gone. Are you interested?"*

"Was I interested?" says Ian. Even now, all these years later, his eyes sparkle at the memory.

Melcher knew what this assignment would require. Asking Ian Berry to go would guarantee that, if at all possible, there would be top quality images of not only the "hardware" of the invasion but an in-depth and sympathetic account of the civilians caught up in the conflict. If the Czechoslovak Uprising went the way of the Hungarian one, this would be a People's War. That Ian would, somehow, be able to dodge the authorities and remain invisible was what Melcher hoped for.

Unbeknown to Melcher, Don McCullin had flown to Vienna hoping to take the popular, and shortest, route to Prague. This was the preferred route but McCullin found himself in a log-jam of journalists, kicking his heals at the Austro-Czech border. While editors fumed and cursed, demanding copy, little could be done but wait. Czechoslovakia was sealed tighter than a drum.

Ian Berry had been ready for some time, and all he had to do was grab his photographic kit and go. But, there was a problem: his visa had expired. Anticipation is a good skill for a journalist to possess. As Don Quixote said: *"a man who is prepared has half fought the battle!"* The trouble comes when you over-anticipate. Obtaining a visa early seemed like a good idea, at the time. Now, there was only one thing to do and that was to race across London to the Czechoslovakian Embassy, to smile sweetly at the officials behind the desk and hope to obtain a new one. The Embassy staff were only too happy to provide Ian with the requisite documents.

With his photographic kit, his passport, a new visa and the accumulation of 35mm film, Ian arrived at Heathrow Airport by 11:30am, only to discover that all the flights to Vienna were fully booked!

Once again, fate dealt Ian a hand he could play, though he ardently denies the existence of a good fairy, a guardian angel or even fate. Mulling over what to do next Ian met a fellow journalist, one who worked for the BBC. This friend suggested Ian fly to Munich instead. This would offer an alternative, though longer, route. It would mean hiring a car at Munich airport and having a more tiring drive, but it would be worth a try. As luck would have it, the next Munich flight had vacant seats. What was there to lose? At Munich airport Ian hired a VW Beetle and was on his way towards the Czechoslovak border.

Though the drive was long, Ian made good time. Trouble came when he arrived at the German-Czechoslovak border and his progress was abruptly halted by the intransigence of the Czech border guards. A coterie of fellow journalists, hanging around the border post, had warned him that to proceed further was futile. They suggested he wait with them in the nearest tavern.

Ignoring this glass-half-empty advice, Ian approached the border control. Faced with similar situations in the past Ian had usually managed to find a way to continue with his assignment. As he waited for his visa to be inspected Ian notice that overall control had passed to a single Russian officer. There were armed Czech guards standing in the background but they did little more that look menacing. Had there been just Czech guards there might have been a chance, but with a Soviet officer it would be impossible, surely.

The day was fast losing its light and warmth as Ian wound down the window.

The Russian officer approached the car and leant into the window to inspect the documentation. Much to Ian's surprise the officer spoke passable English. From the way the Czech guards were reacting it was obvious they did not. Perhaps, thinks Ian, this was the reason the Russian officer was so accommodating; he felt superior to the Czechs and wanted them to know that. Rubbing their collective Czech noses in his superior Russian education allowed Ian to pass himself off as a delegate at the Prague Architectural Conference. On the flight from Heathrow, Ian had read an article about the forthcoming conference and now he sat amidst a squad of heavily armed guards pretending to be a delegate whilst the back of the Beetle was full of photographic gear.

But it worked!

Prague, Czechoslovakia
An embarrassed Russian soldier is harangued by Czechs in Wenceslas Square

On his way to Prague

Ian was waved on, the barrier was lifted and he passed through the Iron Curtain.

"When I told him I was attending this architectural conference all he had to do was check my kit. The collection of cameras and lenses should have given the game away, but he chose to believe my story.

"I will never know why the Russian let me through. Perhaps it was a chance for him to exercise power over the Czechs. Regardless of the reason, I was on my way to Prague."

Ian Berry

Once through the checkpoint Ian found himself lost in the back lanes of the neighbouring town. What were the chances of getting into Czechoslovakia only to find himself in trouble because he was driving a German car with German plates in a country that had suffered so much under the German occupation. The horrors of the occupation would still be vivid in the minds and memories of many of the citizenry. Irony of ironies if he should manage to penetrate the Iron Curtain only to fall foul of the local population.

Unable to speak Czech, Ian was apprehensive about approaching any of the locals. He eventually summoned up his courage and charm and tried to converse with one of the friendlier looking ones. Instead of the expected antagonism, he soon discovered that, yet again, he had landed on his feet. This was an area where ethnic Germans were in the majority and where German was the dominant language. Without hesitation Ian was directed through the town and out onto the road to Prague.

Prague

Arriving in Prague meant finding a safe place to stay and somewhere he could park the Beetle away from prying eyes. It would also need to be sufficiently close to the action for Ian's purposes. The city was in chaos: all the shops were closed and in daylight (the following day) it seemed the whole of Prague was out on the streets. Arriving in the dark did provide a chance for Ian to sleep. Once he found an ideal hotel all he could do was bed down for the night. It was unfortunate, though hardly surprising, to find the hotel empty of both people and supplies. Searching the kitchen, hoping to find something to eat, Ian was disappointed. There was nothing. Even now Ian has little in the way of excess body weight. He is, and always has been, "slight". Back then he was even "slighter", which meant that his next four days in Prague were an enforced dieting, with Ian sustained himself with little more than water.

Ian had the chance to witness the occupation virtually from the start. Amongst his photographs there are several of tanks rumbling through the night-darkened streets. In daylight, those same streets were full of people confronted by and, in turn, confronting the Soviet armour. Every potentially strategic position in and around the centre of Prague had been occupied.

Concentrating his attention on where the protestors were most voluble, Ian placed himself in and around the main thoroughfare that led down from the iconic equestrian statue in Wenceslas Square. It was here that Ian set to work with his camera. Mature citizens stood side-by-side with fashionably dressed youths; workers and students stood next to intellectuals and elderly grandmothers. Scattered throughout the massed ranks of protesters were those holding placards carrying messages of hope and protest.

About the citizens of Prague, Ian said *"They were very helpful and seemed to be unanimously against the Russians. There were lots of tanks on the streets surrounded by Czechs shouting insults, to the confusion of the Russian soldiers. Half the Russian troops were Asians, with Russian officers; they didn't really know where they were - most thought they were in Germany - or what was going on."*

One of the most telling of Ian's photographs was captioned by *Paris Match: "Why are you here?"* The soldier has his back to a wall and is surrounded by a crowd of Prague citizens. Ian was close enough to capture the pain and anger on the faces of the Czech people and the embarrassment of the soldier. The picture also shows how physically close the people felt able to approach their occupiers.

It is doubtful whether any of the young conscripts could have answered that question. It was not for them to argue the pros and cons of the *Brezhnev Doctrine* nor consider the rationale behind *Communism with a Smiling Face.* For many of them it must have come as a great surprise when confronted by an articulate, passionate and well-educated population, and to discover where they were and what was expected of them.

Adept at avoiding trouble (a skill he honed in Africa when confronted by the South African Police) Ian exposed roll after roll of 35mm film. Loading black and white high-speed film into his cameras, he moved in and around the action. Being a man with a couple of cameras hanging round his neck marked him out as an obvious target for Russian anger, though most of the time Ian hid his cameras hidden beneath an oversized overcoat. When he did attract the attention of aggressive Russian officers, Ian's escape was invariably followed by abusive shouts and gunfire, the latter, thankfully, passing over his head. It was at those times that the citizens of Prague came to his aid yet again. Through trial and error, Ian found his best method of escape was to run towards a solid wall of protesters. Time and again, a pathway would suddenly open up and, like Moses smiting the waters of the Red Sea, he could pass from view only to have this corridor close immediately behind him, the protesters coming together and once again linking arms.

On other occasions, running down one of Prague's many darkened alleys or along a narrow street to escape the pursuing Soviet forces, an anonymous hand would reach out from the shadows and haul him into the darkness of a safe doorway. It was then that Ian would remain silent and still whilst the echoing tread of the pursuing, heavy-booted soldiers ran past. It was only when those footsteps faded away that the grip on him would be loosened.

There was always the hotel to return to at night. Safe it may be, offering a place for him to sleep, yet there were still no staff nor was there any food. It remained so throughout Ian's stay. He existed on water until, on day four, Ian was given food by sympathetic locals.

Back out on the street, in daylight, it became clear that the Russians were tightening their hold. Whereas the Soviets had assigned 31,500 troops and 1,130 tanks to the suppression of the Hungarian Uprising in 1956, over 200,000 troops and 2,000 tanks had been sent into Czechoslovakia.

Crowds continued to gather around the statue of Good King Wenceslas and make their linked-arm walls of peaceful protest. People climbed upon tanks whilst others tried to remonstrate with individual soldier. Young people gathered to whistle and jeer, whilst younger boys threw stones at the tanks, only for the Kalashnikov-armed troops to dismount and chase them. The noise of protest became a counterpoint to the rumble and crunch of tank-tracks on cobbled surfaces. Then, as Ian moved amongst the crowds taking photograph after photograph, he could see the faces of the people hardening into masks of despair and resignation. With so much firepower and all the troops not understanding much of what was said to them, it was fast becoming clear that any residual hope for a more humane government was fading. Time was running out for both the Czech people and Ian.

News filtered through that some of the protesters had been killed. Ian made his way to the mortuary to see for himself. There, resting on a mortuary slab, was the body of a young man who had died from wounds received when hit by a Russian vehicle. This was Milan Kadlec, a 20-year-old toolmaker with the Prague Public Transit Company. Milan was just one of several who died that first day, 21st August 1968. Most of those killed on the day the troops arrived died close to the radio station. Of the others who died, they had usually fallen victim to the poor driving of the invading forces, though some had been deliberately shot. As well as the 20-year-old Kadlec, a 72-year-old woman died when a tank knocked her, and a customer, over as she stood at her street corner newsstand. This old lady was Bozena Vesela.

There were other photographers in and around Prague, but not many The events in the legislature and other venues were covered by Czech photographers. The one other photographer who was in the midst the action on the streets was, in Ian's words, *"an absolute maniac who had a couple of old-fashioned cameras on string round his neck and a cardboard box over his shoulders, who was actually just going up to the Russians, clambering over their tanks and photographing them openly. He had the support of the crowd, who would move in and surround him whenever the Russians tried to take his film. I felt either this guy was the bravest man around or he was the biggest lunatic around."*

This brave lunatic was Josef Koudelka, a 30-year-old from Boskvice. Ian Berry was aware of Koudelka as they both dodged hither and thither. It would be several years before they met and that was only after Magnum Photos arranged for Koudelka to leave Czechoslovakia for London, where he joined Magnum.

Hilmar Pabel was another photographer active in Czechoslovakia at the time of the invasion. He photographed the events for the German magazine *Stern*. Pabel was already in Czechoslovakia working as a stills photographer on the war film *The Bridge at Remagen*. Ironically, during the Second World War, Pabel had photographed the real bridge (over the River Rhine in Germany) as the Allied attempts to bomb it. Now he was photographing the fictitious bridge. The cast and crew took to taxis and made a hasty departure leaving Pabel to make his way to Prague. This exodus was later made into a BBC Radio programme by the actor Robert Vaughn.

Meanwhile, with his rolls of film exposed and needing to be developed, Ian decided to leave. He had a deadline to meet, with *Paris Match*. Thankful to have survived what the Kremlin had euphemistically called "Fraternal Assistance", Ian left Prague with canisters of 35mm film stashed just about everywhere he could find, in and around the Beetle. The little aluminium cans were wedged in spaces behind the headlights; stuffed into gaps inside the doors and tied behind the hubcaps.

The trouble with not eating is that the body will, eventually, make it clear it has had enough. The food the citizens of Prague had provided, though welcome, was hardly sufficient to sustain him. It could only be a matter of time before Ian would have to pay the price for all his frenetic activity. However, it was illogical to remain any longer in Prague. There was only so much good fortune he could count upon and, by then, there was a slow trickle of other photographers arriving. Common sense prevailed and Ian left Prague heading for the border.

Light-headedness led to a lack of concentration. It took a super-human effort to force himself to stay awake. Eventually, Ian did reach the border where he expected his progress to be halted. Driving as normally as possible and remaining calm Ian knew that, should he be searched, the guards could easily discover his stash of film. Appearing as nonchalant as possible, Ian approached the border checkpoint. To his surprise the guards just waved him through. Now the build-up of tension from being behind the Iron Curtain was lifted, Ian's exhaustion asserted itself. Fearful of missing his flight, Ian drove non-stop through Germany only to succumb to his exhaustion and spin off the road into the ditch.

Shaken awake by the accident, he recalls looking down at the car and realising the ditch was too deep to reverse the Beetle out without assistance. There was no way he could do anything on his own. Just when Ian needed that metaphorical guardian angel, a friendly farmer came by and offered to pull the Beetle out of the ditch with his tractor. Was the Beetle drivable? A quick check revealed only a single dent. There was nothing hanging off and the cans of film were still secure.

"I got to the airport only a few minutes before my flight left and to get my film I had to rip out the headlights, door lining and hub caps and throw them in the back of the car. It also had a big dent in the side where I had gone into the ditch, but there was not a word of complaint from Avis."

Did Ian meet his *Paris Match* deadline? He did! The two editions of the *Paris Match* magazine that concentrated upon the occupation of Czechoslovakia were number 1008 (31st August 1968) and number 1009 (7th September 1968). You can still find them. Paris Match has back copies or you can hunt through eBay. When I obtained my copies, I told Ian that I was surprised he had used colour film. He said he hadn't, so I showed him the colour photos from both covers. It seemed that the editors at Paris Match very cleverly coloured their covers. This was back in 1968 and we thought photographic jiggery-pokery started with photoShop!

1970 and the trip of a lifetime through Africa

1970 was the year one of Ian's friends, Jimmy Fox , a Magnum editor, managed to secure a major commission for him. *Encyclopaedia Britannica* required a photographer to produce a sequence of storytelling images for a series of educational film strips. Ian knew Africa and had won the coveted Encyclopaedia Britannica award for best photographs two years in a row. He was the ideal choice.

Once he had agreed to the story, Ian began looking at the logistics of the assignment. It became clear that the best, and most cost-effective, way to complete the tasks would be to drive himself from venue to venue. Soon after Magnum was founded one of its founding members, George Rodger, had embarked upon a similar, long-distance drive through Africa. George Rodger's work is much admired by Ian and the chance to emulate him was too good to pass up.

Fortunately, the subjects Ian was commissioned to photograph were all scattered along the west coast. This meant he could concentrate upon the workers, artists and their jobs, both urban and rural in a coherent, in a single trip. The brief also allowed Ian to take his time whilst doing it. The rub was that it required him to dedicate a few months to the project.

Not a problem! Ian was keen to go and even found a kindred spirit in John Gale, one of the *Observer's* journalists. John would accompany Ian and send regular reports back to the *Observer*, each one would record their progress. This meant Ian would have someone with whom to share the driving. It all sounded ideal.

Next came the transport. Ian was advised to purchase a diesel Land Rover. "Very reliable!" he was told. But, when he enquired (with the intention of purchasing one), he was told there was an 18-month waiting list. As it so happened there was an alternative: a six-cylinder, long-wheel-based, petrol-engined Land Rover that was available for immediate sale. For those who know anything about Land Rovers the four-cylinder engines are what the company usually fit. Having a six-cylinder petrol engine is a rarity. Still, Ian could ill-afford to wait for 18 months and, besides, the Land Rover was already being modified to a Dormobile configuration. This would allow several people to sleep in it and cook meals. The roof had a section that could be raised to permit the occupiers to stand up, and provide an additional sleeping area for children. With advice as to how to adapt it to suit rugged conditions, Ian set about obtaining extra wheels, jerry cans for petrol and other items. Everything looked set.

Two weeks before they were due to depart, John Gale contacted Ian to tell him he would have to back out. His 16-year-old son had become involved in a spot of bother with a much older woman. There was every possibility that the son, James, would be named in a divorce case. At this point Ian suggested James came along with them. An extra pair of hands would be useful and they needed a cook.

Being a man of perspicacity and being methodical as well, Ian had made sure the Land Rover was not only suitably equipped but everything that could be a potential problem had been given a thorough inspection and overhaul. Everything should be fit for purpose would be.

Apparently not!

What should have been a trouble-free drive down through the Iberian peninsula turned into a nightmare. The Land Rover would travel for 100 miles so and then stop, refusing to go any further until it had rested. Prior to the trip, Ian had assumed that an official Land Rover garage could be trusted to make sure everything was in tip-top condition. It was only when a local mechanic investigating the problem, discovered that a flexible valve, one that sat snugly in the carburettor, had been fitted upside down that the trouble was fixed.

This trip was made in 1970 when independence from colonial rule was still new and, in some cases yet to be achieved. The political climate they met in the various countries could be volatile and unpredictable. Neither Ian nor John Gale had any illusions that the trip would be plain sailing. There were bound to be problems along the way. Perhaps it comes as no surprise that there were problems.

Travelling Ssouth in Morocco, they were skirting the western edge of the Sahara Desert. Ian had been advised to obtain special lengths of track to place beneath the wheels should the Land Rover become stuck in soft sand. These supposedly essential items collapsed the first time Ian was forced to use them.

Anyone who spends time with Ian knows that there is always at least one camera somewhere about his person. On every occasion I have been with him he has a camera bag slung from his shoulder containing more than one.

John Gale in his memoir of the journey, *Travels With My Son*, paints pictures of halcyon moments of sitting by the Land Rover eating Marmite-covered biscuits as they watch an eagle circling overhead. Ian remembers it somewhat differently. Unused to facing the unexpected and coping with anxiety, Gale's perception of events sometimes make those events seem a wee bit more dramatic than they are, says Ian.

In Spanish Sahara (now Western Sahara) someone, Gale says, deliberately sent the trio in the wrong direction and they became lost in the scrubby, flat desert. After a futile search for the track, quartering on the compass, they settled down for the night.

James Gale cooked dinner and they sat under the stars listening to the BBC on their radio and contemplating what to do next.

"Suddenly there came a voice in the darkness, and a man walked into our circle of light: an old man in blue rags and blue turban. He seemed to want something, though it was hard to make out what." Travels with a Son. (1972) John Gale published by Hodder & Stoughton

What he wanted was a box of matches. Having seen no one for most of the day, to have this stranger suddenly appear as if conjured up by Aladdin and his magic lamp was unreal. Eventually they understood the stranger wanted matches. Taking the box gratefully, the Tuareg listened as they mentioned the town they were heading for. Thinking for a brief moment and consulting the stars he put his two hands together and pointed in a particular direction, saying: "Nouakchott."

After this one utterance he departed back into the dark desert as mysteriously as he had arrived.

In Mauritania, then still under French administration, Ian was persuaded to tow a vehicle owned by a Frenchman, whose wife was sick. Ian's concern was for the Land Rover. Too much stress upon the half-shaft might cause it to break; he was at the beginning of the journey and hadn't yet taken a picture. He had invested a great deal of his own money in purchasing and adapting the Land Rover, little wonder then that he feared for its safety.

Anyone who earns their living using a camera is in constant fear that a vital item could be lost, stolen or damaged. Should damage occur and there just happened to be a store close by selling the missing parts, then all would be well. Not so in North Africa. As for the many rolls of film, these required a safe and cool place in which to be stored. Normally, a refrigerator of some kind is best for keeping the rolls of film safe. Once again, the facilities of the Land Rover had to suffice, in this case a wardrobe converted by Ian with its insides transformed with foam and its outside covered with reflective tinfoil.

Theft of kit is the curse of a photographer's life when on the road. Many of Ian's fellow photographers have had bits of their kit stolen. Ian has been mugged a couple of times but has, so far, been relatively fortunate. In South Africa, he was mugged by a couple of Africans who threatened him with a rusty, very unhealthy-looking breadknife. Ian had no intention of trying to pit his small, utility, do-everything Swiss Army knife against two large guys who possessed such a large and potentially infectious weapon.

"I know lots of colleagues who have lost lots of stuff. I take my bag down to breakfast with me in the morning. I don't leave it in the room and, especially not in New York. Lots of people have lost stuff there.

"I've been mugged a couple of times: in South Africa, in Istanbul and in Peru. When I say mugged, only in South Africa was it physical." Ian Berry

Whilst in Peru to cover a Festival, Ian lost an exposure meter when a patch pocket on his jacket was slashed across the bottom by a person using a razor blade.

Arriving in Dakar after days in the desert, the trio were filthy. The Land Rover was just as dirty outside and in. The back door let in sand and dust. The joy of Dakar was that is was a typical French town offering a hotel with a bath, hot water and a restaurant. *"Total luxury."* said Ian.

Looking for a thank you gift for Jimmy Fox (the Magnum editor who negotiated the assignment for Ian), Ian sought out an African carving. He found what he was looking for in a shop in Dakar. It was the ideal present but the trip had hardly begun and there was always the chance that, should he buy this carving, it might well get broken, let alone add to the weight. After thinking hard about it, Ian came to the conclusion that it would be best to delay the purchase. This was Africa, after all, and there would surely be more opportunities to buy a carving nearer the end of the journey. Ian left it. Even now, all these years later, he still regrets not buying it when he had the chance. What was available later on was either airport trinkets or just tat. It was only towards the end of the trip that Ian found a piece he felt was suitable and on which he spent an exorbitant amount. This carving was purchased from a museum.

Moving through Senegal to The Gambia, the trio arrived just in time to experience the Republic Day celebrations. From The Gambia, a narrow country surrounded on the three landward sides by Senegal, they re-entered Senegal, this time its southern part. Arriving at the border control they received a courteous welcome though the official suggested they follow the vehicle in front rather than make their way independently. To their surprise, they found themselves caught up in the extensive peloton of the *Premier Tour International Du Senegal*. John Gale said *"The French may have gone, but Le Cyclisme remained."*

In Senegal, Ian had two assignments. One was to photograph a local shopkeeper of the Wolof tribe whilst the second was to photograph a hospital clinic in Pikine

Of the main assignment John Gale wrote:
"Ian had to show the family's life, and he spent hours at the shop, which was a small tin shed with a narrow counter in a sandy alley. [If Ian spent hours there it was because he] was painstaking and conscientious."

The next problem facing the trio was a lack of a direct route to Mali. Their aim was to head for the capital Bamako. Unfortunately, the only viable option was to drive to Tambacounda (in Senegal), load the Land Rover upon a flatbed railway truck thence to be shipped by rail to Bamako.

The Land Rover was placed upon the flatbed, roped for security. Ian reflected: *"We were left to enjoy the ride (if that was possible) seated in the vehicle. This was, after all, a goods train. The train set off and travelled for a brief while before stopping in the bush, in the middle of nowhere."*

The trio waited, and waited... daily exposed to the relentless sunshine and heat while still expecting the train to depart at any moment. Every request for information was met with a philosophical shrug. Whilst they sat on the flatbed the local goats gathered for a mass chew of the ropes. With every gnash of a goat's jaws the security of the Land Rover became more and more tenuous.

Having dissuaded the goats from chewing through the ropes, the next problem for the trio was obtaining food. Heat and boredom contributed to the sense of abandonment but that was hardly anything compared to the lack of food. The only sustenance available was fruit, so their diet became fruit and more fruit. Exceeding their five-a-day had a disastrous effect upon their digestive systems. Stuck on the flatbed, fearing should they move that the train would depart without them, they had none of the necessary facilities. Resorting to the best solution they could think of, they took turns in squatting over the far side of the wagon.

Thankfully, the train eventually moved off and headed towards Bamako. Here, Ian's task was to photograph a milk factory. Upon arrival in Bamako, they were forced to wait for two days before the Land Rover was unloaded from the flatbed. Once the Land Rover was unloaded they were able to drive into the centre of Bamako.

Mali proved to be full of frustrations. In the middle of the city they found themselves entangled with a troupe of East German jugglers rehearsing their act in the street before a large crowd enjoying the free performance. To add to the surreal nature of their stay, Mali had broken off diplomatic relations with the British because of the situation in Rhodesia, therefore, there was no British Embassy. A comment made by Gale at the time upon the situation they met in Mali was that *"Mali is an extraordinary mixture of socialism and corruption"*.

Mauritania
Travelling through West Africa on assignment for Encyclopaedia Britannica in a Land Rover, the vehicle is parked in the middle of the desert for the night

Ian's assignments were straightforward. He was to make the story from the point of view of a milk factory's technician and his family. Once that was completed, his brief was to drive to the north of the country, to Djenné, a town of grey mud, where his subjects would be two men of the Dogon nation: one a mask maker and the other a farmer.

Assignments completed, they journeyed on to the Ivory Coast. It was at the Mali border control that they fell foul of the local bureaucracy. The position adopted by the border police had a certain logic: they had taken the train from Senegal to Bamako and had entered Mali at a point where there were no border police. Therefore, they had no entry permit with the necessary entry stamp. That was logical. However, without an entry stamp, the border police told Ian they could not issue an exit stamp. That was logical.

"This is not in order!" said the border policeman. Having entered Mali via the freight train they had no proof of entry. Using his incredible diplomatic skills and charm Ian managed to persuade the policeman to allow them to travel onwards, into the Ivory Coast. In the Ivory Coast, Ian was to concentrate upon logging, more specifically the transporting of the cut logs as they were floated down the river.

Another assignment completed, they travelled on to Liberia. When they reached the Ivory Coast's border post the officer warned them *"Liberia is Texas, main ce nest pas gentil."* And so it was!

Liberia had declared its Independence in 1847 though it was not recognised by the USA until 1862. The settlement began as a move by the American Colonisation Society to provide a home for free Black Africans and Black Americans, an alternative to remaining in slavery or living free in the United States.

It was late afternoon when they left the Ivory Coast checkpoint and drove the short distance to the Liberian Border Post, thus being in effect in no-man's-land. The three Liberian police were dressed in a fashion reminiscent of the American police, complete with dark glasses and attitude. The border was closed and to cross, it needed an overtime payment. *"There are three of us,"* one of these officers said: police, immigration and customs. *"Give us $20 each and you can go."* They made it clear they were not going anywhere and neither was the Land Rover.

Not being the sort to succumb to bribery, they refused to pay. The consequence was a thorough search of the contents of the Land Rover. Ian was ordered to empty it. Once all the gear was laid out for inspection the border guard didn't bother to spend any time looking, merely ordering them to put it all back. The price was still $20 each.

They slept in the vehicle and tried again in the morning, assuming there would be no overtime to pay. It was the same: $20 per person. Once again they were forced to unpack, then made to put everything back. The price remained the same: $20 per person. There was to be no option but to pay.

Everything cost money in Liberia. Ian was to photograph a local fishing family. The first fisherman took Ian out in a dugout canoe for six hours. The trip was not productive, save for Ian being sick for five of the six hours of the trip. On landing, the fisherman took Ian's money then disappeared. Ian needed a fisherman with a family so they continued to search for one.

While out at sea with the new fisherman, John Gale, a man with military experience, had become embroiled in an argument of some sort with the local governor. The immediate consequence of which was the confiscation of the Land Rover. Talking with a Dutch trader whose local knowledge they respected, he suggested they had only two alternatives, either to pay the exorbitant sum the governor demanded or hire a plane and fly to Monrovia (the capital) and obtain a letter from the president. Not wanting to pay the governor, Ian was on his way to see the president. President Tubman was curtesy personified and offered Ian tea and biscuits, and a letter. The two-way flight did, indeed, cost less than the amount demanded by the governor.

The next stage of the journey would take them to Sierra Leone.

Once in the country they headed for the capital, Freetown, determined to visit the hotel where the British writer Graham Greene stayed during the Second World War. Greene had been posted there as an agent for MI6, British foreign intelligence, having been recruited by his sister Elizabeth.

Kumasi, Ghana
Tribal chiefs with gold headdresses attend the funeral of the old Asantehene, Otumfuo Nana Osei Tutu Agyeman Prempeh II on 27 May 1970

Kumasi, Ghana

Mourners attend the funeral of the old Asantehene, Otumfuo Nana Osei Tutu Agyeman Prempeh II on 27 May 1970

When they arrived, they discovered he hotel, run by a Swiss gentleman, was regarded as as "not very good!" This would seem to be a somewhat diplomatic description. How a nation with a reputation for being the world's best hoteliers could produce the world's worst was (and still is) beyond Ian's ken. Perhaps that was why he was running a hotel in Freetown.

What helped lift their stay above the normal, apart from the dreadful conditions, was their arrival coinciding with the delivery of a fresh batch of Carlsberg beer. The beer attracted customers like bees to nectar and the consignment was drunk quickly, before it had a chance to go off. Such eagerness may have contributed to the behaviour of two German guests. Well into their cups, they mocked James Gale's long hair and called him "a lady". The situation might have spiralled out of control when John Gale confronted them. However, the two Germans decided that the odds were weighted against them when Ian joined the two Gales. They chose discretion over recklessness and backed off.

Ian's concern was, once again, to keep the Land Rover safe, and to this end he had locked it away in a compound. Their sleeping arrangements were far from salubrious. Ian had the unique pleasure (or diversion?) of a large hole in his bedroom wall, through which he was the unwilling spectator to the antics of his neighbour in the room next door... with his pet monkey.

The assignment in Sierra Leone was to photograph the life of an iron ore miner and his family at Marampa.

For the next assignment they were to travel back into the Ivory Coast to photograph a story about a male nurse, who was the district medical officer at Eboué. It transpired the nurse had few, if any, medicines and resorted to injecting people with a syringe full of water. He had a pet monkey in a cage. When the monkey became sick, the nurse resorted to his universal remedy and duly injected it with water. The monkey died.

It was here that Ian caught malaria and the nurse once more decided to use his "tried and trusted" method (of injecting water). On the plus side, the water in the syringe was relatively fresh. Ian spent hours asleep in the back of the Land Rover. Fortunately, Ian survived. It was during this period of Ian's insensibility that neither of the other two thought to renew the entry permits to Ghana.

Surviving the malaria and with the generosity of the Ghanian border controls allowing them safe passage, Ian was back on his feet and photographing the work of a bronze caster. Ghana offered a cornucopia of subjects. The bronze was being cast in Kumasi, the main city of the Ashanti heartland. Whilst there, Ian covered the death of the Asantehene (the equivalent of a tribal king). The funeral rites were followed by the accession of a new Asantehene. Otumfuo Nana Opoku Ware II was the newly crowned Ashante king. His reign lasted until 1999.

The bronze caster Ian photographed used the age-old lost wax technique. From Kumasi, Ian went on to Accra to photograph a dance teacher and, also whilst in Accra, a civil servant. It was at this point John Gale began to feel his job in London might be under threat and decided to return home. Both John and James flew back to Heathrow leaving Ian to continue on his own.

Now alone, every mile of the driving would be Ian's, for whom the next assignments were all in Cameroon. The problem in getting there lay in not being able to drive through Nigeria, that was physically possible, it was Ian himself. Being *persona non grata* in Nigeria he was forced to find an alternative route. The only way for him to reach Cameroon was by ship, and the only ship available was an East German freighter. After negotiating his passage, the Land Rover was winched aboard and stowed on the deck. As Ian was the only passenger no special arrangements were made. There were to be no concessions. Devoid of even third class travel, Ian spent the journey living on black bread and cheese. Still, it was less deleterious to his digestive system than a diet solely of fruit.

The captain and crew were competent and the journey might have been a peaceful interlude were it not for the alarm sounding in the middle of the night and the crew racing to abandon ship.

Not fearing for his own life, what was uppermost in Ian's mind was the thought that the sinking ship would take with it his precious Land Rover along with the stack of film. On deck, it was obvious that the size of the swell and the unsteady nature of the ship were making any attempt to launch the life boats difficult, if not impossible. Watching the crew as they struggled to launch the boats, did nothing to fill Ian with hope for the future of any of them. Relief came when the captain called a halt to the frantic activity telling his crew (and Ian) that it was all an unplanned and unannounced abandon-ship practice.

The Cameroon photoshoots were varied. From photographing a seminary to covering a hospital in Mokolo (run by the Seventh Day Adventists), and photographing a potter of the Bamoum tribe working in Foumban, to visiting a school in Bafoussam, Ian travelled throughout the country. When he went to the area of the Mandara tribe to photograph the work of the blacksmith it transpired that the blacksmith also doubled as the local witch doctor. This, Ian says, made for a good photo story and also introduced him to a mask-maker. It was in Foumban where Ian eventually found the carving for Jimmy Fox. By now, Ian was tired. Whilst the Gales had been there Ian had been saved from cooking and negotiating with the subjects he was to photograph. As well as all that support, John Gale's French had helped to smooth the way on several occasions.

The events of the past weeks would fade by comparison with what awaited him after he entered the Central African Republic. It was there that he was arrested.

The Central African Republic had gained its independence from France in 1960 and had spent many years experimenting with the vagaries of various autocratic rulers. In those post-colonial days, what passed for the administration of justice could be somewhat eccentric. On this occasion, Ian was arrested as a spy upon entering the market place. Very tired and feeling peeved at the corrupt nature of the region, Ian drove himself, along with his police escort by his side, to the prison. It wasn't long before it became clear that, as usual, his freedom would cost.

For four days Ian was locked in a cell with several other Africans. It was a small room with a bowl in one corner for the calls of nature and what passed for food was not only virtually inedible but was served in a communal bowl and had to be eaten with their unwashed fingers. This incarceration remains seared into Ian's memory. Eventually, he came to an agreement with the prison governor and was released.

With his Land Rover intact he headed for the Congo.

By now, Ian was in a mess. He had not bathed for some time and the conditions of his confinement had only added to the layers of muck. Being a man in need of a shower, (if not a bath) Ian was grateful to be offered both a shower and edible food by the staff at an American mission. Clean and tidy, Ian looked forward to a well-deserved rest but this was a short-lived illusion. On the second night at the mission, he was informed that the man who had placed him in prison and whom he had bribed to obtain a release, was on his way to demand more money. There was little he could do other than make a hasty exit.

The road to the Congo led to the border town of Bangui and the river crossing over to the township of Zongo. The Ubangi River is a formidable barrier to anyone wishing to cross. Back then, in 1970, it was even worse. There were no bridges and the passage was by a single ferry, and that was broken. It lay on the far bank with a hole below the water line. There was little alternative but to improvise.

The presence of a collection of native pirogues gave Ian an idea. He hired several of these river craft and lashed them together. Pirogues, being locally made small boats, are also ideal as they tend to be of a uniform size. With local help Ian found a couple of planks to place over the dugouts, upon which he could rest the Land Rover. Despite the fragile nature of his craft, and being unsure if it would be sufficiently strong, Ian had to make the crossing. There was no other choice. He had no way of knowing how far behind him the prison governor might be.

Just before Ian loaded his Land Rover onto the improvised vessel, he was approached by one of his helpers who told him of two Germans, travelling in same direction as Ian, who had recently crossed over and been attacked upon their arrival at the far bank. Not only that but all their gear had been taken. Hoping to prevent the same fate, Ian employed a local man to ferry his fuel and other loose gear across the Ubangi and to guard it on the far bank.

As the Land Rover (and Ian) made their way across the river he was surprised and more than a little annoyed to see the newly employed guard of his gear paddling back. Obviously, his pile of loose kit would be vulnerable. Fearing the fuel and the other loose items might have been taken Ian was overjoyed upon landing on the Congo side of the river to see his kit all there, unguarded but intact.

That time of the year was the wet season. When rain came it fell in a dense curtain making driving conditions appalling. The roads were dirt tracks at best but the rains turned them into rutted mud slides. Even in a Land Rover Ian's progress was slow and, if that wasn't enough, he was finding food virtually non-existent. Compounding the problems of the journey there were rumours of armed rebel forces in the area. Meeting a couple of Frenchmen, Ian was warned there were rebel forces up ahead and they were armed, but had no ammunition. *"Just go!"* was their advice.

Bearing this advice in mind, on the two occasions when the rebel *Force Police* tried to stop Ian, he just put his foot down and kept going. Thankfully, it was only abuse they could hurl at him and not bullets.

The state of the road never improved and Ian was glad of the kindness of the local Congolese. In one of those never-solved mysteries, whenever the Land Rover became stuck people would somehow emerge from nowhere and help to push him free of the mud. The real problems were from the traders. Those who Ian approached were mostly Greek and unwilling to sell him anything because he didn't have any Congolese currency. What he was most in need of were refills for his petrol cans... and food. Once again, there was a very limited range of food to eat. For Ian, the choice was either plantains... or plantains. For those of us who have survived by eating cooking bananas we know that no matter how it is cooked it can still be like eating balsa wood.

From the Congo, Ian arrived at the Ugandan border and never, throughout the trip, had he felt so pleased to see a border force. This was before Idi Amin became president and the soldiers manning the border controls were smart, polite and efficient. Not only that, but the hotel Ian stayed in was run by a fellow Lancastrian and provided hot water for a luxurious bath, along with quality soap and good food. For the duration of his stay, Ian had *"a great couple of days!"*

With the assignments completed and the road ahead relatively straightforward Ian, now suitably refreshed, travelled on to South Africa.

Though the assignment for the *Encyclopaedia Britannica* had been completed, this was far from being the end of his journey. The next issue for Ian to resolve was how to get home, especially with the Land Rover.

Tanzania
A Masai youth huddles in his blanket against the chill of the morning mist while protecting his cattle armed only with his spear

The journey home

Once more, the heavy hand of bureaucracy conspired to cause delays. There were problems with visas. Being 1970, and this being the time when, because of its policy of apartheid, South Africa had declared itself a republic and left the Commonwealth, none of the countries Ian would have to pass through had representation in South Africa. By now Ian's family had joined him. His wife and their two children were all set to accompany him on the drive back to London.

"We thought it would be a good experience for the children. All that wildlife would surely be an attraction, but they were blasé about them. They had seen them all in the London Zoo." Ian Berry

From Johannesburg, Ian drove up to Mombasa. The plan was to take the Land Rover and the family by ship to Karachi. That meant driving to the port of Dar es Salaam to board a freighter. Whilst many of the ships could accommodate passengers, it was transporting the Land Rover that restricted the choice of vessel to another East German freighter.

From Karachi, the road they took led south, out of Pakistan and into India. The aim was to spend Christmas in Goa. Goa had been an overseas territory of Portugal until 1961, when it was annexed by India. Goa's situation on the Western Ghats and its biodiversity along with the many attractive buildings and nightlife made it a desirable venue for a holiday. It was also a favoured destination for many of those who experimented with the then prevalent counter-culture. Ian's photographs of Goa show the skinny, pale complexioned hippies with their sarongs, long hair and colourful headbands.

Back in the early 1970s there were various hippy-friendly places: Morocco, Bali Thailand, Nepal and Goa were favourites. Life could be lived cheaply and, sitting on a beach was an ideal way to watch the world go by, as you tried to "find yourself." Then again, there was the sea which was always warm and inviting. Idyllic as this might seem to Ian and family, London beckoned and they had to move on.

Far from finding India a total idyll, when they reached Hyderabad Ian was, thankfully, helped by staff at the American Embassy to take the children to a local hospital. They had both contracted a serious eye infection. The children were confined to a darkened room for a week. The symptoms were so bad that there was a fear that their eyesight might be permanently damaged, and Ian and his wife were very scared for their welfare.

Eventually, with both children on the mend, the family continued on their journey home. From Hyderabad Ian drove to Benares, now better known as Varanasi.

Ian's 1971 photographs record the sacred River Ganges at Varanasi with a classic Ian Berry image of two boys and a white cow caught in the benign warmth of the golden evening light. But it is the water and the ritual bathing that dominates the Varanasi photographs. There is one in particular which shows one of the pilgrims photographed from behind, praying in the evening light.

From a photographer's point of view, Varanasi was a joy. Even better was their next place to rest and refresh themselves. It was the disputed territory of Kashmir. For the length of their stay they spent time on one of the many decorated and fantastical houseboats moored on one of the lakes. Here Ian resorted to his favourite black and white film. One of his juxtapositional images places a veiled woman to the left of the frame, dominating the picture and there, in the background is a flock of white and grey geese. Another Kashmiri photograph is of a child leaning out of one of the houseboats looking at a duck that is swimming past.

Time passed all too quickly. Now the ever-beckoning road left Kashmir and headed back towards Pakistan. This was still the early months of the year and travelling in the mountains brought with it all the joys of a winter journey. As is the way with such off the beaten track journeys there could be no predicting what you would come across and, often, these encounters could be of a surreal nature. Travelling down a relatively steep mountain track in the Himalayas Ian and family encountered the strange sight of a 2CV Citroën travelling towards them... backwards. It was being driven, if that is appropriate, by *"two crazy Frenchmen".* Granted, the 2CV was trying to negotiate an icy slope, one which the Land Rover managed with great ease. Thankfully, the Land Rover was suitably equipped with a set of bull-bars on the front. The result was inevitable: Land Rover 1, 2CV 0.

On another occasion, the bull bars proved useful when Ian was faced with a temporary stone wall hastily put up across the road during a border dispute. Though it was only several layers of loose bricks and not that high it was, nevertheless, sufficient to stop most of the traffic. Experience had taught Ian the wall had been built for some nefarious reason, one that probably involved money. Not one to suffer such interference readily, Ian decided that, rather than wait till someone came to do what they intended, he would just drive on. What with bull bars and a serious four-wheel drive vehicle built for such situations, he had no trouble in surmounting this obstacle. The trouble was that the driver of the next vehicle in the queue felt encouraged to follow. This was a poor choice. This vehicle was not a four-wheel drive nor did its have sufficient clearance to cross the remains of the barrier. This vehicle, occupied by a friend travelling in tandem with Ian, became grounded on the rubble. Ian rushed back, shouted at the other men to help him shift the debris. Many of them came to Ian's aid though not all. Some of those who refused to help even went as far as to throw rocks through the windows. All this happened on the road which led to Peshawar.

At one stage, during the drive along this road, Ian and his family were only 50 yards or so behind a large American vehicle. Tragically, this car ran over an old man. In such circumstances the customary (and sensible) advice was not to stop but to drive on and report the incident to the nearest police station. In this case the outcome was not so clear cut. The local people were far from forgiving and chose to open fire on the vehicle as it drove away. Further down the road, Ian and family came across the car riddled with bullet holes and abandoned by the side of the road. Giving it a cursory look Ian was satisfied that it was now less of a vehicle and more of a colander. As for the passengers, Ian never discovered what happened to them.

Afghanistan, though still an "interesting" place to visit, was certainly not the Afghanistan it is now. However, this was the home of one of the biggest hippy fashion icons: the Afghan coat! Initially from the *Ghazni* province, between Kabul and Kandahar, it was give the Beatles' seal of approval when they wore them for the *Magical Mystery Tour* album and film. Though available in hippy boutiques on London's Kings Road since 1966, owning a truly genuine one would be such a coup. Ian bought them for the children.

Before the journey, Ian's choice of a petrol engine Land Rover rather than a diesel engined vehicle had been derided by those of his acquaintance who were supposedly in the know about such things. However, Ian felt a degree of satisfaction when petrol had been so readily available throughout the trip and diesel had been scarce.

At an Afghani filling station the garage attendant filled the Land Rover's petrol tank, but with kerosene (also known as paraffin). Whether this was a genuine misunderstanding or not will never be known. What we do know is kerosine is suitable for heating and cooking with (or fuelling an aircraft's jet engine). It has no place anywhere near a road vehicle. Kerosine burns at too high a temperature. Not knowing what had happened Ian drove off. The heat from the fuel igniting in the six cylinders destroyed some of the engine valves. Miraculously, the simple fact that the Land Rover had six cylinders rather than the customary four, meant it continued to run, though with less enthusiasm when it came to hills and rough terrain.

The family left Afghanistan and continued to travel through Iran, still with only four of the six cylinders working. Speed was naturally reduced and the Land Rover needed a daily push-start to get it going. Regardless of where they stayed, the early morning ritual of pushing the Land Rover always attracted suitable volunteers. This was not a problem in both Iran and Turkey. There, the citizens were only too willing to push. On some occasions, even members of the army joined in. However, by the time the family crossed into the then Yugoslavia, there the only people who offered to push also demanded payment for doing so.

Chugging on, further into Europe, they were now reduced to a mere 30 miles per hour maximum, even on the flat and tarmac roads. Until they arrived in Austria there had been little or no chance to have the Land Rover looked at. In Austria, they found a Land Rover agent who was certainly able to repair the vehicle but whose advice was that the cost would be very high, much higher than in London. Because the Land Rover had travelled such a long way in this damaged state (albeit slowly) why not continue thus. From Austria to London, the family Berry chugged along the roads of Europe at a steady 30 mph.

The concerned photographer

One of the characteristics shared by the early members of Magnum Photos was a concern for their fellow man. The *Family of Man* exhibition, curated by Edward Steichen, then director of the Museum of Modern Art in New York, opened in 1955 and displayed many images from Magnum members. These images typified the humanitarian nature of their work. Those founders had all come to maturity with a left-wing sensibility. In fact, much of the early work of Henri Cartier-Bresson, David "Chim" Seymour and Robert Capa was printed in the French magazine *Vu*. This was a very socialist publication owned and edited by Lucien Vogel. The magazine had witnessed the rise of fascism in Europe and strived to make its readers aware of the growing threat. The work of the founders of Magnum Photos set the template for much of the future work of the co-operative. Not only was it a cornerstone of its members it was also one the was firmly held expected to be adopted by any of the new member.

This was the pre-existing ethos which Ian embraced when he became a Magnum member. It is probably not surprising to those who know Ian that he was accused (in the nicest possible way by the committed socialist Philip Jones Griffiths) of being a self-confessed *Hampstead Liberal*. It is only natural, as you look at Ian's work, that it reveals him to be a proactive humanitarian, and a concerned photographer.

Mexico

Guatamalan refugees live in squalor near the Mexican border, hoping for a better life

Slavery

Mention the word "slavery" and images of African men and women being dragged along in chains may be what spring to mind. Surely, it died out in mid-19th century? Apparently not. It has become a topic of recent concern because the horror of enforced labour and all that that entails is as current now as it was back in the 18th century, along with the curse of human trafficking. The word itself, "slave", can generate a mental image, one that shouts of emotional damage, of theft and transportation. The image that probably most readily springs to mind is of shackled bodies, locked away in a fetid hulk, being shipped across thousands of miles of wild ocean only to be sold as a commodity, labour, and worked to death. These conditions were vividly portrayed in the Spielberg film *Amistad*. Perhaps the fetid hulks may be less prevalent these days replaced by refrigerated trucks, but the corruption of slavery is, sadly, all too real.

If we believe slavery to be a thing of the past, sadly this is not so. If anything, the curse of modern slavery is more widespread than in the early 19th century, before legislation outlawed it. Current estimates place the number of slaves at 27 million worldwide (Kevin Bales, President of *Free the Slaves*). Other estimates put the figure higher. Concerned that something should be done, a group of people came together to highlight the problem, to bring the issue to a wider audience. In 2007, a coalition of the Hayward Gallery (its Touring section), Autograph ABP (the Association of Black Photographers) and Magnum Photos was formed with the aim of producing a touring exhibition of photographs which would focus upon various aspects of modern slavery. Lending its considerable weight to the project, the Magnum photographers who became involved each had a reputation for reportage of the highest quality. Included amongst the eight Magnum members was Ian Berry.

The title of the exhibition was *Documenting Disposable People, Contemporary Slavery*, and with lottery funding and support from other charities, a book was published to accompany the exhibition. Ian's brief was to look at the situation as it existed in Ghana. The title chosen for Ian's section was *From Slave Trade to Trade Slaves*. In his introduction to Ian's section Kevin McCullough, then global campaigner for Special Initiatives at *Christian Aid*, detailed the problems caused by international trade and the power of international financial institutions.

The Ghanaian section traces the shift from a country that was self-sufficient when 70% of its population **earned** their living from agriculture, (McCullough) to a country that, in a short time, came to be dependent upon foreign imports. To obtain aid and support the Ghanaian Government had been forced to open its markets to foreign goods. At the same time it had to stop giving support and subsidies to its own farmers. For those 70% of Ghanaians whose livelihoods depended upon agriculture, this was a tragedy. It was to report on the outcomes of this shift in policy that Ian went to Ghana.

Travelling from the rice growing region in the south of the country, to the tomato-growing region in the Ashanti North, and the poultry farms in Kumasi, Ian documented the growing hardship faced by these once-successful farmers. His work showed that the problems faced by one sector of a community would influence the community as a whole. In most cases it was the labourers who were no longer needed and, with a reduction in the wages, the viability of local shopkeepers suffered, along with others in the supply chain: the packers and shippers and delivery drivers.

Cheaper goods flooded the local markets: cheap imports of Italian tinned tomatoes brought ruin to many of the tomato farmers, pricing them out of business, is just one example. McCullough quotes a tomato farmer, Kofi Eliasa, who was ruined and forced to find alternative work to be able to feed this family. From being a successful tomato farmer supporting more than his immediate family, Mr Eliasa was forced into taking one of the only vacant jobs in the region:12-hour a day breaking stones in a quarry. For this, he earned less than $2 a day. In a sequence of photographs, Ian shows this once proud tomato farmer using simple hand tools to crush stones into hardcore.

The ripple-effect from these farm closures resulted in Kofi's children, like so many others, being unable to attend school where a simple payment was needed to provide each pupil with pencils and the like. Many families in similar positions left the land and moved to the cities, hoping for a better life but finding few opportunities when many others followed the same path.

Ian's photographs reveal the imbalance. Cheap and subsidised rice from the United States flooded the markets in Ghana. Arguably, cheaper rice would benefit the consumer, but with reduced wages and a struggling urban population, the impact upon the Ghanaian rice farmers was disastrous. Once an exporter of rice to neighbouring countries, Ghana became an importer and Ian's photographs highlighted this. As a form of slavery this may seem esoteric, but the indications are there: the inability to continue with a sustaining occupation; having to move and find work of a very demeaning nature and being beholden to a "master".

During this assignment, Ian heard of the practice of some fishermen buying young children for $20 and a bottle of whisky each. Compared with a story about bags of rice this seemed to be a story more immediately relevant to the theme of slavery. Travelling from Accra north to Lake Volta, Ian met George Achibrah who worked to free the young boys, who had been sold by their parents so that the family could survive. It was a case of too many mouths to feed and not enough to go round. The boys worked for no pay and were being deprived of an education. With his typical non-judgemental approach, Ian manages to show the human cost of modern slavery and its endemic place in some societies.

In one of life's ironies the vital need for clean water persuaded charities and the government to install community taps as a viable and cost-effective remedy. The availability of clean water might, on the surface, appear to be a major step forward. In Ghana, for example, it became readily available. This access to clean water with all its health benefits is a cause close to Ian's heart. With this in mind you would expect him to celebrate this Ghanaian development, and he did photograph people gathering to collect water, in Accra, the capital. However, his research discovered a sting in the tail. The water utilities were privatised and prices rose, limiting access to water for poorer communities.

As is Ian's practice, he concentrates upon the activities of individuals and shows their trials and struggles. There are photographs of tomato farmers walking along their rows of plants dressed in rags. Ian photographed the fishing boats nestling under the white walls of the 17th century Cape Coast Castle. This is no accidental shot. The castle protected the most lucrative and active slave port in Africa, one that was originally Portuguese but later British.

The *Disposable People* exhibition started at the Southbank Centre in September 2008. It moved on to various UK University venues and Art's Centres culminating in Aberystwyth in January 2010. Ian's story about the child slaves, *Sold into Slavery* was published in a French edition by CDPEDITIONS, August 2008.

Refugees

With only two weeks in which to photograph the plight of refugees in makeshift camps in each of the Central American countries, Ian worked on a story that would be used by the UNHCR. It was when he photographed the Guatemalan refugees, who had gathered in the Mexican coastal area of Campeche, that he felt compelled to stay with them as they prepared to return home. His first view of the conditions under which they were living contributed to this decision. He felt that, to do these refugees justice, he would need to accompany them. It was a sudden decision and he had no time to equip himself better. So, with only a small rucksack and a couple of fruit bars, he set off to walk to Guatemala.

For two days they walked through thickly wooded country and over mountainous terrain. There were no bridges, and the rivers and streams they encountered had to be waded across.

"It was all a bit miserable," says Ian. It rained the whole time. The widest river was waist deep but *"you want to keep your Leicas out of the water".* One of the telling photographs Ian made at the time shows a woman and her children huddled for shelter under a battered sheet of rusty corrugated iron.

Catania, Sicily

The Cattedrale di Sant'Agata provides a corner of sleeping spaces for young women who have nowhere else to go. Here, one slumbers despite the constant flow of tourists past her resting place

Water

When you consider the number of major waterways Ian has travelled along, let alone the stream and the minor water channels, here is another potential book just featuring those travels. He has photographed the Thames, the Mekong, the Rhine, the Nile, the Mississippi, the Ganges and the Yangtze along with many more. But these are important highways providing work and access and trade as well as being a source of power.

There are smaller, more intimate rivers and creeks which serve the same purposes but on a smaller scale. There are unseen sources of water which provide Ian with very human stories. These small, human-sized sources offer interactions of an intimate nature in which the people bathe and cook and clean. Whilst projects like the Three Gorges Dam on the Yangtze provide spectacular photographs it is invariably the domestic aspects of these smaller water sources that interest Ian. For so many of us, turning on a tap and having clean water gush out is something we take for granted. Should there be a problem there is usually someone who can come and sort it out for us. In this way our continued good health will be assured. We pay our utility bills and they promise to keep us supplied. This may be a universal right, a universal expectation but it is not a universal reality.

This is being written at a time of great climate shifts. Drought and floods are everyday items on the news. Rain falls where little or no rain has fallen before. At other times and in other places farmers and industries are taking water to "feed" insatiable urban demand, whilst others are finding a lack of water makes their land unsustainable. As time passes we are being faced with the realisation that water is a finite resource, unlike the power supply where we can invest in renewables and alternatives. Where once we feared there would be wars over oil supplies, shortages of water may present a more pressing problem.

As populations grow and the weather patterns change even "wet" countries like the United Kingdom could well face serious water shortages in the future. Some informed speculators put this as happening within the next 15-20 years. We are all living in a time when weather patterns have become unpredictable. The hot, dry British summer of 2018 may become more the norm. This may be great for some but not so good for others.

The British are seen as a nation obsessed with the weather. This may be true as we may not know from one day to the next what we will be faced with but taking an inexhaustible supply of water for granted will no longer be possible. No wonder Ian takes recording the world's water as a serious, and very personal, project.

Water, and the ability to access it, becomes a factor in games of geopolitical diplomacy. Politics aside, there are parts of Africa and Asia where a shortage of water (and sourcing it) becomes a matter of life and death. Yet, in other countries, where there is an apparent abundance, the problem becomes one of access to safe water.

One country which has featured large in Ian's articles especially about water is Bangladesh. Ostensibly Bangladesh has an ample supply of fresh water fed, as it is, by waters from the mountainous regions to the north of the country. Yet, this apparent abundance of water is being reduced by the dams being built closer to the sources of these rivers in neighbouring countries.

Generations of Bangladeshi people have relied upon this abundance and have taken it for granted. To change the habits of a lifetime takes time and an adequate infrastructure.

Finding a source of clean water then building a safe and easy way of accessing it is often the aim of many of the NGOs (the aid agencies). However, this all costs money and, using Bangladesh as an example, this may be one expense that is low on the list of the country's priorities. Teaching good hygiene practices becomes essential, but even that is an additional cost.

In Bangladesh, a low-lying country prone to flooding, the answer would seem to be drilling deep wells to source clean water from below any flood-induced contamination. This is a seemingly simple answer, yet it is constantly thwarted by the continuing fall in the water table. This is due, in part, to the building of those dams already mentioned. These dams feed the growing needs of the expanding populations of the neighbours but do little for Bangladesh, which is at the end of the river system and can only expect the "left-overs".

Outside observers may be forgiven for assuming Bangladesh has been blessed by a surfeit of water in its streams and rivers. Contrary to accepted logic, this excess has become yet another part of the problem. When you expect an annual bounty of water from monsoons and the like, there is the tendency to take it for granted and dismiss any possible problem. Yet, the bountiful annual supply becomes relied upon for a great many purposes. It becomes the answer to everything from bathing babies and drawing cooking water to leading cattle to rivers for them to drink (and to defecate in). This domestic use does not include the demands of the various revenue-generating industries. Bangladesh's reliance upon manufacturing cheap clothes pollutes water sources with a cocktail of chemicals and dyes. The production of cotton cloth alone places great demands upon the river systems.

Low-lying countries close to the seas of the world face the inexorable rise in sea levels. The consequence of this is the intrusion of salt water into what was once productive fresh water. This corruption of the "fresh" water makes that which was used by coastal farmers impossible. In 2009, Ian photographed the effects of this spread of saline water onto Bangladeshi farmland. The regions surrounding the river Padma were once fertile and produced a surplus of rice, to the point where it was exported, adding much-needed cash to the Government treasury. This is no longer the case. The salt water makes rice growing impossible and now the farmers are forced to turn to shrimp farming as an alternative. Rice is now imported and adds to the national debt whilst the shrimp farming does little to ease the situation.

The NGOs dedicated to providing clean water have been very proactive, building standpipes and deep wells. In many cases, though, the lowering of the water table has rendered some of these unusable. You would assume that all you need to do is drill deeper. Not necessarily. Those managing to pump water to the surface are often found to be polluted with high levels of arsenic. Of Bangladesh's population of 160 million it is estimated that at least 20 million are at risk when using these arsenic-polluted wells. In an effort to keep its population safe, the government colour codes its wells. Polluted wells are painted red and safe wells green, yet the people still find it necessary to source their water from the red wells. This is not simply a matter of education. In many cases it is Hobson's Choice for there is often no other source available. Ian photographed a group of women holding their hands out to show the dark marks on their palms, an indication of arsenic poisoning.

While people drink the water, the levels of bilharzia continue to rise and children die of diarrhoea. In Bangladesh 62 children in every 1000 under the age of five contract the illness. Yet there is a simple, single dose of medicine available that could alleviate many of the problems caused by bilharzia but this requires a local medic to ensure a repeat dose is taken. In most instances in areas difficult to reach, this cannot be guaranteed.

Africa revisited

Ian spent part of 2003 working with the charity Medecins Sans Frontieres (MSF), in Burundi and Rwanda. There, the work of the MSF was mainly focused upon counteracting the effects of malaria. Ian photographed the health centres where MSF was working. Anopheles mosquitoes breed in stagnant water. Uncovered water sources attract the mosquito where they go to lay their eggs. It is imperative to give the local population access to clean water that is larvae-free. This means the digging of safe wells and the fitting of pumps. However, even after such water sources were provided, there were still those who insisted on taking their drinking water from sites like Lake Kivu. Ian's photographs show women washing their children in the lake alongside others drawing water for drinking and cooking, as animals follow them to drink, and do what animals do.

In one sequence of harrowing photographs, Ian charts the increasingly virulent hold malaria has on one man who is waiting to be seen by the doctors. In one frame he falls flat on his back, and lies inert. The medical staff carry him to a cot and attach an intravenous drip to hydrate him. He lies there with the other malaria sufferers, who are mostly children and young mothers.

In 1987, it was Ethiopia's famine that Ian photographed. Using both colour and black and white film, Ian's lens covered the tragedy that was unfolding. His photographs, especially the haunting portraits of children waiting for a meal along with the emaciated patients, the cholera victims and those with malaria, are all shot in monochrome in such a way that each frame concentrates upon the pain and suffering, allowing each patent to retain their dignity and quiet resignation. This is evident of even the youngest victim.

Ian returned to Ethiopia in 2007 and his photographs from that visit show a very different country. In those 20 years the atmosphere of and condition within Ethiopia have changed. This time the majority of Ian's images are in colour and show a vibrant society, one which was beginning to stand upon its own feet. Amongst Ian's photographs are images of village clinics where the adequate stashes of medicine are being stored in freezers. There are other photographs: panoramas of the lush green of the Berga wetlands and environmental portraits of the Addis Ababa Women's Association making and growing and selling their produce. There are images of fashionable Ethiopian youths in restaurants and others of traditionally dressed members of the Pathfinder Women's Empowerment Group feeding bird-watching visitors from America's Sierra Club.

Typically, Ian also seeks out the unusual and humorous and on this visit, at Boricha Worida, he photographs a man on his way to a family planning meeting. Nothing unusual in that you might say, but the man is carrying a very sharp, polished spear! The potential in this image for writing a humorous caption is very tempting.

Abidjan, Ivory Coast
A woman contributes to a colourful scene in the township

Zululand, South Africa
Zulus on their way to celebrate a wedding

Belfast, Northern Ireland
Small boys lark about at a demonstration in support of H-Block hunger strikers with coffins painted on the pavement

Zones of conflict

Ian Berry has not been immune to some of the twentieth century's darkest events.

Northern Ireland

Northern Ireland in the middle of the Troubles was not the healthiest place to be, especially if you were from "The Mainland" (England). Ian was there is 1981 wending his way amongst the streets regardless of whether they were Protestant or Catholic. His coverage of bottle-throwing and the manufacture of molotov cocktails put him very close to the action, especially when you remember he is using prime lenses only, and none of them are telephoto (a 35mm and a 50mm mainly).

One of those typically Ian Berry images is of a young boy, perhaps eight or nine years old walking down a road with his face masked and carrying a lance that is twice his size. He is on his way to take on the British Army.

Ian was there at one of the most volatile of times in the history of Northern Ireland. On 1st March 1981, Bobby Sands, a member of the Provisional IRA, had started his hunger strike. In a strange twist of fate, the Independent Republican MP for Fermanagh and South Tyrone Frank Maguire had died suddenly of a heart attack leaving his seat vacant. On 9th April, the imprisoned Bobby Sands was narrowly elected as the new MP. Whatever the motivation, Sands never took up his seat and remained in prison. He died on 5th May 1981.

When Sands' death was announced there were several days of rioting. A milkman and his son died as a result of injuries sustained after being stoned by rioters in the predominantly Nationalist area of North Belfast.

The Coroner's verdict was that Sands had starved to death of his own volition. His death was deemed to be self-imposed. The verdict seems to skirt the word "suicide", which would have been anathema to any Roman Catholic. In the Houses of Parliament in London Margaret Thatcher, the British Prime Minister, reiterated her Government's stance that Mr Sands was a convicted criminal who chose to take his own life, adding that it was a choice that his organisation did not allow to many of his victims. Around the world the stance of the British Government was condemned.

Into one of the most potentially dangerous of situations (for an Englishman), Ian made his way to photograph Bobby Sands' funeral. Prior to the funeral, Ian chose to stand in front of Republican supporters as they hurled objects at the security forces. Some of his other images capture the growing tension as citizens gathered to demonstrate in support of the H-Block hunger strikers, and masked youths stepped up their harassment of the police and army.

On the day of the funeral, Ian captured the sight of thousands of people lining the road to the cemetery and then thronging past the coffin to pay their respects, which was carried by Provisional IRA members dressed in combat clothing, anonymous, with their faces covered by ski masks. To provide the images he thought would best capture the "feel" of the moment, Ian placed himself only feet from the crowds, and recorded the pain on the faces of the mourners. Political funerals where tensions and emotions ran high were nothing new to Ian. His experiences in South Africa had placed him in many a similar and difficult position.

Londonderry, Northern Ireland
Having captured the ringleaders (left) soldiers then move in on the mob with batons and rubber bullets

Belfast, Northern Ireland
Men hurl rocks and molotov cocktails at the security forces in the prelude to Bobby Sands' funeral

Ian had been to Northern Ireland ten years earlier, in 1971, following the British Army as it patrolled the streets of Londonderry. This was a story which provided Ian with one of those dilemmas often faced by photojournalists. The youths in the area where the unit was patrolling had gathered to throw stones at the army patrol. The bulk of the patrol formed a wall with their shields and slowly retreated down the road. The youths followed. This was the oldest trick in the military book for, unbeknown to the lads, a snatch squad was hiding out of sight, in a doorway.

Once the youths were abreast of the snatch squad, it pounced and grabbed the leader. It was then that the troops took this unfortunate youth to one sided and *"Kicked seven bells out of him".* When seeing such blatant aggression the photographer is presented with a moral dilemma, what does he or she do?

Ian Berry's problem was not only what to do but when he attached himself to the unit his presence had given rise to initial suspicion. In one of those strange twists of fate he had been accepted on the say-so of their sergeant. This sergeant recognised Ian from the Congo, where he had served as a mercenary.

Having made the connection, Ian had been welcomed into the troop. Their subsequent actions were their natural behaviour for a patrol. Ian was accepted to the point that their treatment of the youth had been photographed, and those images were incriminating. Whatever he decided to do he would be betraying one side or the other.

Before Ian could do anything an officer arrived and the incident was resolved. Yet, Ian still had images unfavourable to the conduct of the British Army. What should he do with them? Initially, these images were going to the *Daily Mirror* newspaper who operated on a "publish and be damned" policy.

Evidently, the pictures were sufficiently damning even for the *Daily Mirror* so they decided not to run with the them. *The Express* was the next port of call. Initially, they said "Yes!" but changed their mind. At this point an agent sent the images to a short-lived publication: *Seven Days*. Ian, back in Northern Ireland, received a message from the agent that it might be advisable for him to come home because he (Ian) would most probably be very unpopular with the British Army. It became clear there was some criticism and a belief that his coverage was one sided. When his images were published however, the incriminating ones were not included.

He was back in 2004 to photograph a different Northern Ireland. This time he was on assignment for the National Trust. The images were of loving couples walking along the beach in Antrim and lobster fishermen lowering their pots. Visiting birdwatchers were photographed standing on the sea cliffs concentrating upon the myriad of nesting birds. And outside Cushendun's General Store in Antrim, a group of boys are photographed as they decide what they can buy with their joint finances. This is all very peaceful. You feel that this is what the boys should be doing, instead of filling milk bottles with petrol and lobbing them at British troops.

The Vietnam War

This was cat-nip to many journalists and it was another conflict that Ian spent time covering. Philip Jones Griffiths had remained in Vietnam for some time but wanted to come home to edit his film. Ian was available and assigned by the *Sunday Times* to photograph the effects of defoliation by the use of Agent Orange. This time Ian was paired with the writer Nicholas Tomalin (1931-1973). Well-regarded as a writer and voted by his fellow journalists as one of the top 40 journalists of the modern era, Tomalin was to die in Israel when reporting the Yom Kippur War.

The two men, decided the best way to assess the effects of *Agent Orange* was to fly over the contaminated areas. To this end they needed to hire an aircraft. First one company and then another refused to carry them. While Nick was running around trying to find a flight, Ian found an orphanage of mixed-race babies (called Bui-Doi in Vietnamese which means "dust of life"). The pictures that sold were of mostly coloured babies in cots covered with sacking sheets on which was printed "Gift of America". He also found a prosthetic limb factory when Vietnam, because of necessity, was the biggest and most advanced manufacturer of prosthetic limbs.

As a last resort, Tomalin tried Air America, which was a charter company run by the CIA and, strange to say, they were willing to accommodate the two journalists. The flight itself was relatively uneventful though the photographs and the subsequent story were well received. However, the pilot informed the journalists that he needed to land at one of the CIA's more isolated outposts. The landing strip was a passage cut through the forest by Agent Orange which had then been reinforced with Marston Matting (more properly called pierced steel planking, aka PSP). The landing was as smooth as any landing could be given the circumstances. The CIA team that met them seemed overly relieved. The reason for this was soon apparent when they mentioned that *"Charlie"* (the nickname given by American forces to the VietCong guerrilla force fighting the American-supported South Vietnamese Government) had been active in the night and they feared the landing strip had been mined. Landing safely meant that their fears were groundless.

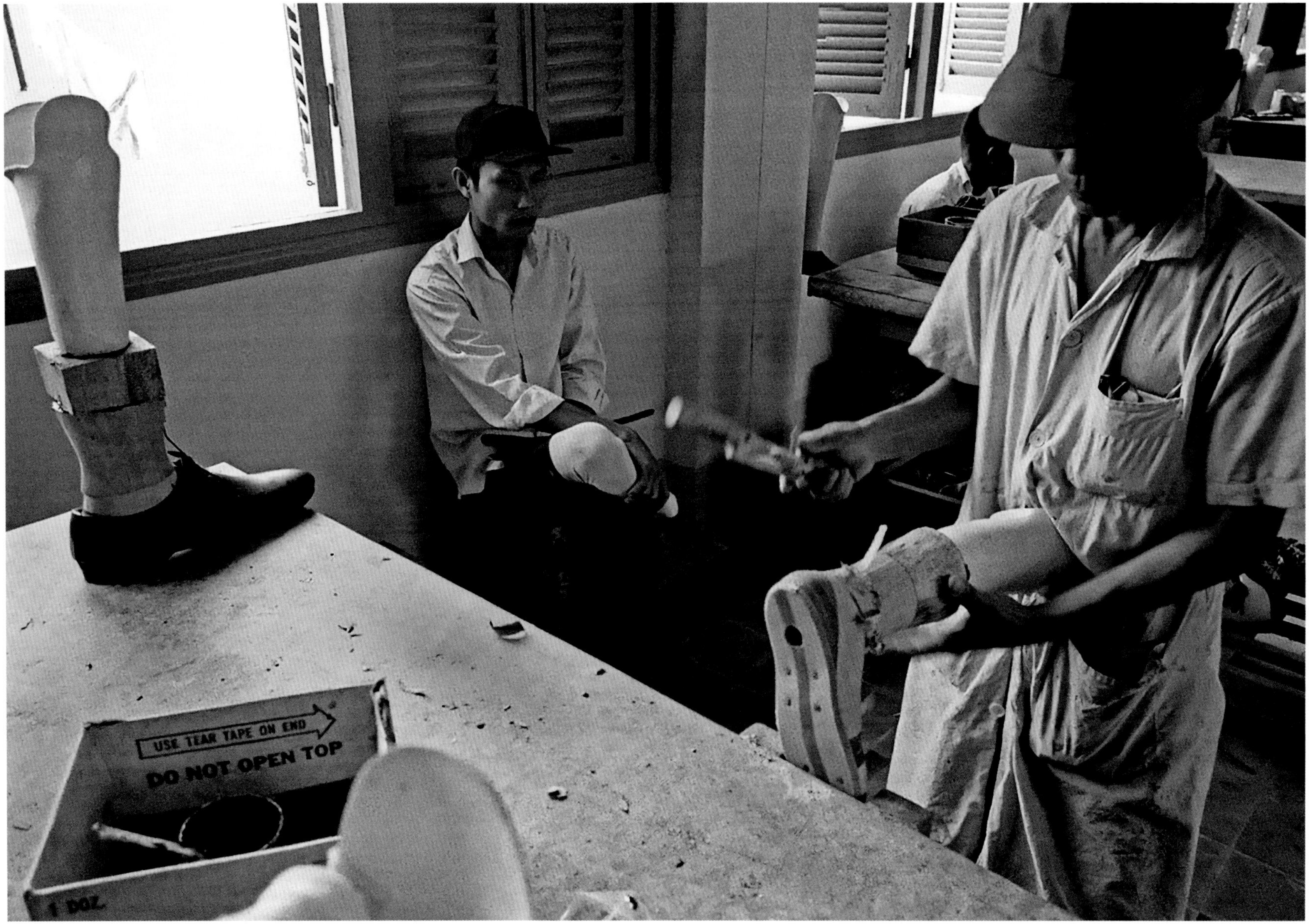

Vietnam
At the time of the Vietnam War, the manufacture and fitting of prosthetic limbs was more advanced than anywhere else in the world

Vietnam
A woman grieves at the funeral of her husband

Israel

Israel in 1976 was the target for much terrorist activity. In July of that year the Israeli Army carried out a raid to free the passengers of Air France Flight 139 who were being held at Entebbe Airport in Uganda. This was a very active time for terrorist activities. Not only was the raid on Entebbe a success but in October of 1976, Israeli Naval Commandoes raided the harbour of Tyre to sink a ship they believed was linked to the terrorists.

Ian arrived in time to witness the Israeli Army at work in the West Bank. Working with an army unit, one which was obviously reluctant to have him there, Ian travelled with them on a halt-track on a mission to remove mines. He was accompanied by a hawk-like PR man to ensure he did not take photographs of the secret weapon that was attached to the front of the vehicle. When not operational this bulky appendage was completely covered by a tarpaulin. Oddly, the only man who seemed not to have a designated role on the vehicle was a Druse Arab.

One thing that you should never say to Ian, let alone any other Magnum Photographer, is, "you can't."

Next day, Ian positioned himself so he could photograph the vehicle coming towards him. The secret weapon was an amazingly complex feat of engineering placed at the front of the vehicle: a tree trunk to which a chair had been bolted. The Druse Arab's job was to sit there and indicate where the possible mines were. It was certainly a cunning plan. Should the poor detector fail to notice a mine or similar contrivance, the consequences of this would be catastrophic, especially for the "detector".

Ian was able to spend time with the Palestinians thanks to the journalist Gavin Young. Through Young's connections, Ian was introduced to the Palestinian spokesperson and legislator Hanan Ashrawi who put him in contact with the mayors of both Nablus and Ramallah. This was a time when the Israel Defence Forces was violently reacting to the throwing of stones by youngsters. In the morning, early, Ian would receive a telephone call from one of the mayors inviting him to breakfast. This sounded benign and friendly should anyone be listening, which it was, but it was also code for Ian to place himself opposite a house that was about to be destroyed. Invariably, the house would be the home of one of the stone-throwing youths.

Another of Ian's contacts was fellow Magnum photographer Micha Bar-Am, a resident in Israel since 1936. Through Bar-Am, Ian obtained his accreditation and was allowed to visit various places not normally open to journalists, one of which was a prison housing Palestinians. To Ian's surprise, when he entered, the inmates were sewing what looked like mail bags. If anything was stereotypical of incarceration it is surely the sewing of mail bags. What next, picking oakum perhaps?

Whitechapel and *The English*

The project that eventually became the book *The English* was a milestone in photography in Britain. For one thing it was the result of the first Arts Council grant awarded to a photographer. For another, it set a pattern for many of the photo books that came afterward.

Ian worked with the BBC on an assignment in the Yorkshire fishing town of Whitby, a town which he would feature in *The English*. His time spent in Whitby coincided with a dinghy race in the harbour and a day of sunshine, both of which he used to his advantage. Climbing the 199 steps from the harbour side to the Church of St Mary and the ruins of the Abbey, Ian was filmed as he moved amongst the sun-bathing crowd, capturing the relaxed mood of a summer, Sunday afternoon.

People were stretched out on the grass at the top of Tate Hill, others walked through the tall grass of the churchyard and each and every one would, eventually, be incorporated into Ian's portrayal of the day. The one that he eventually chose to feature on the cover of the book is of various people sat on the cliff top, which is now no longer there (a storm sent a mud slide down to come to rest on the back wall of the kipper smoke houses lining Henrietta Street). In the distance, you can just make out the "matchstick" BBC cameraman with this tripod.

Jenny Stein of the Whitechapel Gallery heard about *The English* and asked Ian to photograph Whitechapel. This was to be the first photographic exhibition at the gallery. Prior to this, exhibitions had been solely of art which drew an audience primarily from the West End of London. Jenny's aim was to bring local people in to see the images of their own environment. In this she was spectacularly successful.

London, England

Children play on the wastelands of Canary Wharf where a huge regeneration scheme is underway

Ashington, England
Nappies hang on the line in this once thriving mine village

1974: a hectic year, and a typical year

There is no particular reason for choosing 1974. It could have been any other year around that time. What 1974 reveals is that Ian was, typically, out and about, working just about everywhere. He completed a travel article in Yugoslavia, only to come home and walk the very gritty streets of the northeastern British town of Sunderland, photographing those areas of the town where old housing was being demolished. Sunderland is in the middle of the East Durham coal field, though even then it was in the process of contracting. Now *King Coal* is no longer mined. The collieries are all closed, the pithead gear has been dismantled and the men no longer tramp to their shifts, their clogs click-clacking on the pavements.

Sunderland's other claim to fame was that it had been one of the UK's busiest shipbuilding towns. Whilst Newcastle citizens are known as Geordies, those who come from Sunderland are known as Mackems. This is widely believed to derive from the boat-building term: "we mack 'em and you tack 'em" (We make them and you take them). Sunderland was typical of so many manufacturing centres in the region, reliant upon shipbuilding and coal, and the ancillary industries that supplied the needs of these two voracious monsters. The decline in these industries meant it was vulnerable. Sunderland died in those years and it would have to wait until 1984, when Nissan moved to the area along with its servicing industries, when something like prosperity returned. Ten years later and the plant (now the largest in Britain) would produce its millionth vehicle. As I write this the fate of the British automotive industry is once again in the balance as the divorce from the European Union becomes a reality.

Ian's approach to the region was typical of his other work in similar situations as he concentrated upon the people whose lives were being turned upside down. If one image speaks for many it is that of the elderly lady, bent-backed and trudging along a side street of boarded up terraced houses. The street is wet with rain and in the distance at the end of the road is a stark white statue of Christ on the cross. This image, and others from the region would become part of Ian's patchwork portrayal of life amongst *The English*.

Variety can provide the challenges photojournalists thrive upon. As for Ian in the 1970s they came thick and fast. One day he might be photographing Kensington's public laundry, and the next he would be off to Hamburg in Germany to work on a project to photograph the police. Somewhere in this maelstrom of stories was one spent in the Netherlands covering the Dutch fuel crisis. Architectural photo assignments were all part of the work, and Ian seemed to become a specialist in covering the building of airports and, later, covering the airports once they were up and running. Amongst those he photographed during construction were extensions at Heathrow and Gatwick and the building from scratch of Paris's Charles de Gaulle Airport.

1974 brought nearly thirty stories Ian's way, stories as varied as that concerning the once-thriving East Anglian port of King's Lynn and, by contrast, the vibrancy of the city reputed never to sleep, New York. Less hectic stories saw Ian accompany members of the British Army as they visited various stables and stud farms in Ireland as they sourced horses for the Cavalry.

More stamps in his passport in 1974 saw Ian in Italy, then on to Bremen in Germany and Marseilles in France. Not that the year ended in one of the many potentially exotic venue where Ian might be working, but the winter of 1974 saw Ian photographing a story in Milton Keynes.

Ian Berry, an observer of social change

Over the years, Ian has found himself at the forefront of recording social and political change. Often, various magazines will request an article upon a particular phenomenon. One such was a request by *GEO magazine* for him to photograph immigrants and fascists. These stories are best served by photographing the people involved and capturing their actions, reactions and mannerisms. As an example, enter the word *refugees* on Magnum's website and you see that Ian has photographed the plight of refugees for many years and in many countries. That list will include:

Immigrant children in the UK in 1972, in 1976 and in 2011
Central America in 1988
Pakistan and child labour in 1993
Armenia in 1994
Natal (South Africa) in 1994
Immigrants in Berlin 2000
Cambodia (where the refugees are being used in a sweat shop)
2007 Vietnamese refugees in Hong Kong - *The Boat People*

If there is a single assignment that throws a critical (if affectionate) eye over our increasingly diverse society, it is probably Ian's 2011 story of Whitechapel (London). Here we can see modern Britain laid bare for our consideration. Old people in care, the police keeping a measured presence, British Asian businessmen and Bangladeshi market traders alongside Chinese alternative therapy practitioners all plying their trade in this constantly fluid part of London.

There were demonstrations and marches, many of which took place on Ian's doorstep. These ranged from the violence of the Anti-Vietnam War demonstration in front of the American Embassy to the peaceful and orderly anti-nuclear CND (Campaign for Nuclear Disarmament) marches and gatherings in Trafalgar Square. It was Ian's fellow Magnum photographer, Stuart Franklin, who was in Tiananmen Square to capture the famous *Tank Man* image for *Time* magazine, whilst Ian waited for the student protests to spread to Shanghai. The protests spread right across China but unfortunately, not to Shanghai.

One lengthy and serious British industrial dispute Ian covered was that which interrupted work at the Grunwick film processing laboratories. This was one of the longest strikes in British industrial history. It involved a trade union attempt to gain union recognition at the laboratories. It became an often violent strike that resulted in over 500 arrests. It also highlighted the political, social and racial divisions in British society at the time. The strike started in 1976 and lasted two years. One of the outcomes of the dispute was the commissioning of an inquiry led by Lord Scarman. Scarman recommended that both the union be recognised and the dismissed workers be reinstated. The Conservative Party, with support from right-wing groups, rejected these recommendations and when they came to power in the 1979 General Election used the strike as a basis for curbing union powers.

Earning money for Magnum

The financial health of Magnum Photos has been a miracle of hope over reality throughout its 70+ years of life. The collective was partly conceived as a way for those who were earning a living from their photography to help those who were struggling. In the early days surplus money came from any work that could be generated from stories. This usually meant people going and seeking assignments. People like Robert Capa and Eve Arnold proved to be very good at wining and dining clients and securing work. The young photographer Marc Riboud tells how he was taken by Robert Capa to a meeting at the offices of *Picture Post* where Capa talked the editor into giving Riboud a lengthy contract to photograph the state of post-war Leeds (an industrial town in West Yorkshire).

The money these members brought into Magnum Photos kept the collective afloat. Ian, being one of a group of long-established Magnum members (along with Elliot Erwitt, Bruno Barbey, Burt Glinn and Marc Riboud amongst others), was able to bring in the cash. Whilst there were some in Magnum who criticised this group for selling themselves to the corporate world, Ian argues that not only was the money essential to keep Magnum afloat but working with corporate clients allowed you access to places you might otherwise never have been able to go. As an example, Ian tells of his assignment to photograph the New York Stock Exchange. *"Being there for the Stock Exchange opened doors and there were good shots to be had."* On a practical level *"corporate clients pay well and this means you give your children a steady and stable education, provide a roof over their heads and put food on the table".*

The Hitachi Shipyard...

As an example of the classic corporate photo assignment we have selected one that Ian Berry completed for the Hitachi Company. It should have been a simple, straightforward photo shoot for the company's annual report.

In 1972, Ian was on assignment to photograph the Hitachi shipyards. All went well, at first. The company bent over backwards to provide whatever support was needed. This left Ian to carry on with unlimited and free access to every aspect of the work. The workers had been briefed about Ian's presence and told to ignore him. This was the first time in 10 years since a Magnum photographer had provided images for the company.

With his customary respect for the workers and their practices Ian proceeded to move silently from place to place, his Leicas (a quiet camera at the best of times) capturing every subtle aspect of the shipbuilding process. The images were in colour, which favoured the various aspects of the work. Ian's visit to the Honshu shipyard and steelworks would provide him with dynamic views of workers going about their day against a background of industrial hardware. There are pictures of groups of workers enjoying a tea break, others welding and architectural shots of ships and cranes. After a while, though, Ian noticed a change in the attitude of the workers.

At one point, the interpreter accompanying Ian queried why he was working with just a couple of cameras. This, surely, was most unusual?

As the conversation progressed all became clear. Ian was told that the photographer who had produced the images for the company's annual report in 1961-62 was the venerable and iconic Eugene Smith. Smith had arrived with a car full of gear, including

Honshu, Japan
A worker at the Hitachi Zosen shipyard

Honfleur, Normandy, France

Lunch time and the pet dogs are ferried to the restaurant in a baby buggy

Louisiana, America

Early morning on the Mississippi where the paddle steamer, the Mississippi Queen, on its way upriver to Memphis, Tennessee, is moored at St Francisville

a portable drinks' cabinet, a box of cameras and a record player. Every so often, Eugene Smith would seek inspiration and retire to a chair, pour himself a drink and play some music. Ian, on the other hand, moved silently around the shipyard nor was he having inspiration breaks or needing to sit down and listen to music. How could this men be a serious photographer?

The Police...

Another bright idea from the US *GEO* magazine was for Ian to photograph New Scotland Yard, the home of the Metropolitan Police in London. This Ian was happy to do but feared the American *Geo* editor might be disappointed when the images landed on his desk. There was an assumption prevalent in the US at the time that British police would be a motley crew of bowler-hatted, pipe-smoking people reliant upon bloodhounds and intuition andCockney informers. Every case would involve a cut-up body discovered in a suitcase probably left on a platform of some country railway station. Every interrogation would be very gentlemanly and conducted over copious cups of tea.

Hoping no doubt for the various Fabians of Scotland Yard emerging from their oak lined offices into a traditional London fog to cuff the miscreant with the latter exclaiming *"Fair cop Govn'r"*. Poor editor, all those expectations were dashed when Ian's photographs arrived. Instead of dismembered bodies, blood-soaked suitcases and smartly dressed detectives (probably with roses in their button holes) they were faced with the modernity of New Scotland Yard and its various scientific departments. Though Ian's photographs were, as to be expected, of a superior quality, the trouble was that an absence of deer-stalkers, briar pipes and oak-panelled offices did not provide the necessary ambience. Instead, there were computers and all the paraphernalia of a modern police force.

Ian has photographed police forces all over the world and should he gather his collection together these images would be sufficient to fill yet another book.

Starting to archive Ian's collection of police photographs you would need to go back to his time at *Drum*. The images from that period in his life cover many aspects of SAP activities, from heavily armed white officers, riot police and even young recruits patrolling in cars. In fact, Ian spent a night on duty with a couple of young, white SAP officers as they drove around, ironically depending upon Ian's navigational skills to locate their "targets". At one point, over the radio came a call to investigate the theft of a car last seen heading towards one of the townships. The patrol car intercepted the stolen vehicle only to find it was being driven by two African SAP officers supplementing their income.

In Britain, Ian's photographs of the police's involvement with society range from officers containing violence at football matches to confronting those skinheads looking for a fight at the seaside, from the "soft" policing of events such as the CND rallies to being confronted by violence at demonstrations. As documents of social history, these images help illustrate the changing nature of policing Britain from the latter half of the 20th century and into the 21st century.

In direct contrast, Ian's collection of police images includes photographs of armed Italian police officers guarding the mayor of Naples from the Camorra, and the Han Chinese police patrolling the streets of Urumqi in north western China in groups of five or six. That region is predominantly muslim and there is considerable antipathy between the two communities. Still in China, there are Ian's photographs of migrant workers being shepherded by Chinese police officers. In 2007, Ian spent time in New York photographing policemen out on the streets interacting with the population at large.

Ian has witnessed every aspect of the police's involvement with the public, from the violence of South Africa and Northern Ireland to the cheeky attempts to goad the police during the May Day demonstrations of the early 2000s. In 2019, he was outside the Palace of Westminster as the various sides in the Brexit debate confronted each other. Ian Berry has seen it all and recorded it all.

Women...

When you talk to Ian about women it becomes clear that he is a man of considerable experience. Before you run away with the idea that he is a modern-day Casanova, I shall clarify. Like so many of us, Ian admits to having an ideal woman. In Ian's case it is a film star seen on the flickering "silver screen". Back in our youth, we would sit in a darkened cinema, choking from the clouds of smoke that hung in the air between the projector and the screen, tinting the images a subtle nicotine tone. Boys of our vintage looked up in awesome wonderment at those Hollywood sirens. I was very much an Audrey Hepburn fan (Monroe was a little too much for me) whilst one of Ian's favourites was Ingrid Bergman, and who amongst us can be surprised by that. As is the way in Ian's world, The fate conspired to provide him with a chance to meet her.

Thanks to a story for the German publisher, Axel Springer, Ian was asked to photograph Bergman for one of his magazines. Bergman was in London at the time and Ian had the ideal chance to photograph his idol. It was left to Ian to make contact and any subsequent arrangements. This was a tried and trusted procedure and invariably worked well. However, this time it wasn't going to be that easy. At first, her agent said a very definite "No". Ian tried again, but it was still "No". Then Ian sent flowers, and the agent said, yet again, "No". Eventually, having pulled out all the stops, Ian hired a room at the *London Ritz* and a Rolls-Royce to collect her and take her home. This time, either through persistence or the offer of tea at the Ritz, the answer came back: "Yes!"

Everything was ready. Ensuring that the lighting was just so and with both colour and black and white film loaded, Ian awaited the arrival of Ms Bergman.

Meeting your idol so many years after you first became a fan (or infatuated) can result in a conflict of emotions and, sad to say, shattered illusions. The years can sometimes be cruel. When the star of such iconic films as *Casablanca* and *For Whom The Bell Tolls* entered the room, the idol of Ian's youth turned out to be *"a little old lady".* No matter how well she had weathered the years, his dream woman was now 40 years older. Was he disappointed? I asked. *"Perhaps, just a little, but she was wonderful all the same. It was a good session."*

With other women, the photo sessions were sometimes "interesting". Ian was sent to photograph Sophia Loren in Rome but, regardless of how he approached the studio and her agent, the nearest he came to completing the shoot was to photograph Ms Loren's body double. *"Not quite the same as the real thing but she was, nevertheless, a delightful lady and, I believe, she went on to become a Bond Girl,"* said Ian.

Sometimes, Ian worked with an assistant. For two years he had a Swiss woman assisting him, who proved invaluable especially on an assignment for Kodak. It was for a calendar about the River Rhine. Ian's fellow Magnum photographer, Thomas Hoepker, was to work on the landscapes whilst Ian concentrated upon the people. Kodak issued Ian with a stack of release forms and $5 bills. The trouble was that the forms were all in English. This was where Ian's Swiss assistant came to the rescue, explaining to the bemused Germans what the form was for and why they were being presented with American money.

It was Panasonic who offered Ian the chance to photograph on the streets of Rome. The idea was to capture the faces of Romans going about their daily lives, and show how wonderfully the Panasonic cameras worked on the street. At the initial meeting Ian asked about the model consent forms and was told they were unnecessary. Still unsure as to whether this was true or not Ian proceeded with the shoot.

The matter of the model consent forms came back to bite the Panasonic staff on the bottom. They were necessary after all. To make the street shoot and the consent forms viable Ian needed an assistant.

An assistant was duly provided. The girl was a delight says Ian. The only problem was that she was eight months pregnant and the heat was oppressive. Needing the constant support of her partner and ample rests, the girl did what she could and despite everything the session on the streets seemed to go well.

Shenzhen, Guangdong, China
Ancient and modern China come together in a new industrial town

Shenzhen, Guangdong, China
A bicycle factory in Shenzhen, southern China

Flights that were not fanciful...

Ian's connection with South Africa continued down through the years allowing him to chart the changing culture of control. Amongst his archives are shots of white farmers in conversation with African police chiefs and of clashes between white supremacists and white police officers. Perhaps the biggest and most fundamental changes came about when Nelson Mandela was freed from incarceration on Robben Island. Sometimes, his later contacts with South Africans could be somewhat hair-raising. Whilst covering a programme to redistribute elephants from areas where the numbers were causing problems, Ian was accompanied by a fellow photographer. They recorded the tranquillising of the elephants and their transportation. When the time came for the two to leave, a local farmer offered to take them back to civilisation in his light aircraft. This was very kind and they both accepted gratefully.

Once airborne, however, it became clear that the farmer was a good pilot but a poor navigator. They became lost. Circling over the veldt, none of them could pick out a useful landmark. Time passed and any hope of reaching their destination in daylight was fading fast. When all hope seemed lost, the farmer sighted a road and followed it till it came to a crossroads. At this point, he landed the plane on the road, climbed out of the cockpit and examined the sign post. It was this simple navigational aid that saved them from a forced landing in the bush. From then on, it became an easy task to follow the road. Ian's reflection on the event is even now heartfelt, *"Never take a lift from a stranger with a light plane."*

British Gas was a company that returned time and again to ask Ian to photograph various situations and stories for them. One such involved Ian being ferried out to a North Sea platform. Mostly, these stories were completed without any problems. However, there were two stories which provided a sharp contrast to the normal run-of-the-mill assignments. On flight number one, Ian was accompanied in the helicopter by a somewhat rotund BBC cameraman. They were circling over a rig and the BBC man was strapped into a special harness which allowed him to lean out of the open door to film. Having previously agreed to share the time available equally, the BBC man remained filming for far longer than was polite.

With time being of the essence, Ian literally leapt at his chance to take his photographs once the BBC cameraman had stopped filming. The problem was the harness. It was adjusted to cope with a large male (the rotund BBC man). Ian is not large, never has been large and never will be large. In his haste he fell through the harness and found himself outside the helicopter, having passed through not only the harness but also the open door. Fortunately, Ian was dragged back into the helicopter by the second pilot.

The second event of helicopter note occurred, once again, on a rig in the North Sea. This time the event happened as Ian completed shooting on the rig. Ian had an aerial sequence still to do and for this he needed a single-engined helicopter which, having just been repaired, was flown out specially. It arrived and Ian climbed on board. The sliding door was open and Ian prepared to make some last-minute shots of the rig as they lifted off but the co-pilot suddenly pulled him back into the chopper and slammed the door shut. It was then that Ian realised there was silence inside the cabin. Immediately, the helicopter plummeted vertically to crash-land on the helipad. A further stay on the rig was necessary until spares were ferried out and the helicopter was repaired. Understandably, the crew of the rig were unhappy, because a twin-engined helicopter was required to ferry crew and supplies to and from the rigs and with a crashed chopper on the pad nothing else could land until it was repaired and the pad cleared.

Sad to say that Ian Berry's experiences with air travel seem to reflect the sometime dilapidated state of certain ancient and rotting airliners required to ferry people and supplies to isolated sites. The name of one particular airline company is being withheld for obvious reasons. However, crashed helicopters and CIA flights in Vietnam along with the mad dash for a place on the Baku oilfield's shuttle service all make for Ian's colourful cat's nine lives air travel experience. Then again, considering how many thousands of miles he's flown, Ian's journeys are probably the ultimate proof that air travel is the safest of any form of travel.

Magazines and books...

While many of Ian's fellow Magnum photographers were making a name for themselves producing books that concentrated, mainly, upon a single theme (which many still do), Ian was very much a magazine photographer. In one way, it satisfied his wanderlust by offering constant challenges and great variety. The time and commitment to producing a book is considerable and you can spend months making sure the images selected are suitable. One of the other problems is that a publisher needs to be brought on board early in the process. This can be very difficult, especially in today's publishing climate. One of the reasons Ian joined Magnum was *"I wanted someone else to go find the work".*

There is, however, a problem with having your work published mainly in magazines. This can lead to much of it being "lost". Magazines, though regarded as "hard copy" do have a tendency to be ephemeral. With a book however, they do announce somewhat loudly who the author is. They are also a good way to archive your work and owning one can be an investment. For a decent copy of Ian's book *The English* (in paperback) you could be paying anywhere on or around the £100 to £200 mark. Even distressed copies fetch high prices. This is the purview of the bibliophiles who satisfy their obsessions by collecting books on their favourite topic. I am not sure if magazine collectors have the same passion.

When Ian does produce a book the results are spectacular. His *Living Apart* is a classic and, in the opinion of many people, it is a definitive book on South African history in the second half of the 20th century. Ian believes the book on the same theme he produced for a French publisher is more relevant. As for his ground-breaking book *The English*, it is a classic and a definitive record of both time and place. As mentioned above, a near mint copy can set you back over £1,000, though a poor copy would still cost you £90. Poor quality hardback versions can go for about £150.

The *Paris Match* editions which feature his photographs of the Russian invasion of Prague are still available but you have to know what you are hunting for. Other magazine stories come with their own constraints. In one story for the *Observer Magazine*, Ian spent time with the Reverend Nick Stacey in Woolwich (London). It told the story of a progressive vicar in a less than affluent area of London. Rev. Stacey was progressive and worked hard to make the Anglican Church relevant to the people of the area. This included such innovations as installing a coffee bar in the church. The story was shot in 1964 and Ian used black and white film. The Reverend Stacey's work proved to be ultimately unsuccessful and the 6 page article bore the title: *Failure of a Mission*. Unless you have access to the archives, which are invariably restricted, searching for specific images or stories can be both difficult and time consuming, not to say expensive. The only ready source for much of these pieces is from Ian's own archive.

Ian meets deadlines, even when the conditions are dangerous and difficult. He provides good copy that "fits the bill". What more could a picture editor want?

Newsweek magazine has often used Ian and commissioned him to cover a variety of stories. *Newsweek* is an American weekly news magazine which was first published in 1933. Of all the weekly news magazine, it claims to be the one with the world's largest readership (26 million). Most of those readers are in North America. With a mostly text-based output, the photographs are often an important but small percentage of the story. Despite the small number of included photographs, for the researcher, however, they are an invaluable resource.

Having said that Ian's work is not often published in book form, I have to confess that is not strictly accurate. Publishers such as *Time/Life*, the *National Geographic* and various French publishing houses have often asked Ian to provide the photographs for their books. Many of these stories have meant Ian having to travel some distance. One such story involved Ian flying to New Zealand for the National Geographic book of National Parks, but that has already been mentioned. However, some projects were nearer home, such as his contributions to a book *The Sporting Horse* which meant trips around most of Europe.

Sometimes the story can assume a somewhat surreal aspect. In 1963, Ian was working on a story about the Crazy Horse Saloon, the famous Parisian establishment. It was to be a look behind the scenes and it appeared the girls who performed there were quite happy for Ian to photograph them regardless of their state of dress (or otherwise). Setting to with his unobtrusive cameras, Ian made shot after shot and worked until the interval. At this point, Ian noticed a fresh face, one he had not photographed already. Raising his camera, his subject attacked him, both physically and verbally. Somewhat taken aback Ian asked what was wrong. The girl had assumed the worst and thought Ian was little more than a pervert and peeping tom. It wasn't until it was explained to her the purpose behind Ian's presence that she calmed down. What Ian hadn't known was that the performers worked in several clubs and the angry young woman had just returned from a different job not been told about Ian's presence.

One book that Ian was invited to provide the photographs for came as a surprise.

This was in 1989, a time when there was a great deal of trouble between Spanish and British fishermen, especially over quotas and fishing techniques. The invitation came from the Spanish fishing industry. The fact that an Englishman had been asked to participate, especially considering the poor relations between the two countries, took Ian by surprise but he gladly agreed to work on the book. There was one unfortunate (and again, somewhat surreal) incident during the assignment. The various leading lights of the Vigo fishing community invited Ian to dinner. Unable to refuse he went to the feast, which was a celebration of fish. The trouble is that Ian doesn't eat fish. Ian is allergic to fish. To add to the surreal air, it became clear to Ian that everyone around the table was wondering why they had invited this non-fish-eating Englishman to work on their book.

The book must have been a success for Ian was invited to produce a second volume. This time he arrived in Galicia with his camper van.

Accompanying one of the trawlers as it went to sea, Ian wondered about the reception he would get from the Spanish crew. He need not have worried. Once again, coffee assumed its placatory place and sharing a cup (or two) with the captain eased Ian's passage. He was there to photograph the daily routine involved with fishing: hauling the nets aboard, storing the catch and all the other essential tasks. The sea was not the calmest and Ian remained on the deck, mostly lying there (out of the way). He had two cameras with him: a Leica with a 35 mm lens and a Nikon with a 24 mm lens. These were prime lenses and, in the arcane jargon of the photographic world, both lenses were fast which made the capture of movement and any chance shots a possibility. Ian was, by now, using digital equipment. Whilst many of his contemporaries prefer to use a memory card with a high-storage capacity (some even using 32gb or higher) Ian's preference is to use only 8gb memory cards. This proved to be a very sound decision. One of his memory cards was lost. *"Thank goodness, it was only 8gb. Just imagine how many pix I would have lost had it been bigger?"*

Feeling he was on to a good story, one on a firmer footing, Ian went with the women of Vigo as they dug for shellfish. Ostensibly, it seemed to be an easy story to photograph. That is until he accompanied the women to their digging site. Granted he shot some, what to him were, good pictures. What was not so straightforward was having to wade through water up to his shoulders, keep himself steady and upright whilst all the time holding his equipment aloft to keep it dry.

Odessa...

In the early years of the 1980s what was known as the Cold War still occupied a large part of our minds. Though we didn't know it at the time these were the final years of having to decide whether to be 'Red' or 'Dead'. Tourists visiting Russia were benefiting from the twilight of President Brezhnev's lengthy tenure. With his demise in 1982, a change of president invariably meant a change of policy.

In the early years of the 1980s what was known as the Cold War still occupied a large part of our minds. Though we didn't know it at the time these were the final years of having to decide whether to be 'Red' or 'Dead'. Despite Odessa experiencing their last years in the Soviet Union Ian found, once he arrived, little or no economic growth and wide spread poverty despite the Kremlin saying this was "true socialism".

Accompanied by a female interpreter and a male minder, Ian found most things were open to him. Travelling around Odessa being guided as to what was permissible, he was able to keep his Soviet comrades happy and his editor pleased. However, the minders were creatures of habit. "Both the minder and the interpreter clocked off promptly at 5 o'clock. Free to roam, I wandered alone and that's when I took my best photos."

Ian's understanding of Odessa was that it was a Russian city. Everything he was introduced to was described as "Russian". Asked about the fact that Odessa was a Ukrainian city, Ian said it never occurred to him.

Ian was surprised when arrangements were made for him to take photographs of the docks. Odessa was the home of the Soviet Black Sea Fleet and an important port. If there were to be any tension between Ian and the Soviet Authorities, it would centre upon the Black Sea Fleet. The photoshoot was better than expected and after 5 o'clock Ian returned to the docks hoping his access would be still valid. Unfortunately, matters did not go according to plan and he was visited by the authorities who made sure he was on an aeroplane the following morning.

Strangely, Ian returned to Odessa a few weeks later with no obvious problems or restrictions. During his guided tour he had wanted to visit the academy where the national ballet was housed. Before, the minder had kept him out of the academy. Th only issue Ian can think of on reflection is this would have exposed him to Ukrainian culture and people. Alone, Ian made it into the academy and photographed the dancers.

Ian was also able to photograph the School of Stolyarsky, a music school which has an enviable reputation for training many famous violinist such as David Oistrakh.

Odesa, Ukraine
A woman waits oblivious of the drunk passed out behind her

Odesa, Ukraine
In the torrential rain, a woman tries to sell a very small collection of shellfish

Odesa, Ukraine
The onion domes of St Panteleimon church are the background to this passing tram

Stockholm...

For a photographer, Sweden's capital Stockholm is close to perfect as a venue. Ian was there in 1980. The temperature was so low that he was able to photograph men fishing through the ice on a frozen river. Amongst his images of the city, there is one of the city centre caught in a golden hour as the sun sets. With its long shadows there is even one of Ian's trademark passersby silhouetted as he crosses the road.

Walking around the city, looking for situations that he might photograph, Ian came upon a sauna and thought *"What can there be that is more typically Swedish than a sauna?"* Entering the building, he asked the attendant if it would be possible to take some photographs. He explained the background to this request and who he was working with. Asked to wait a minute, the attendant disappeared into the main part of the building. Upon his return, he nodded and told Ian there would be no problem. So Ian entered the hot and steamy atmosphere of the sauna.

The occupants of the sauna who had agreed to allow Ian to photograph them were all women... naked women. Whilst Ian might blush, the women seemed perfectly at ease with the situation. In fact one even invited Ian back for dinner.

Stockholm, Sweden
A sauna and swimming pool for ladies

Still in Stockholm, Ian had approached the police requesting a chance to ride along with a patrol. The request was granted and Ian arrived at the police station late on a Friday evening to be met by the officers he was to ride with. *"They were incredibly good looking and were worthy of being poster cops for the Swedish Police Force."* The woman was blonde and looked like a film star whilst her fellow officer could have featured in a Viking film. The vehicle was a Volvo and when Ian opened the rear passenger door he saw that the seats and everything visible were covered in plastic sheeting. Ah, the thought occurred to him that this might foretell the nature of the night's patrol. He was right.

The task of these two officers was to patrol the streets of Stockholm gathering up those who had partaken of too much alcohol and an excess of drugs. The plastic sheeting was there to save the seat fabric from too much abuse. Regrettably, Ian was not so fortunate and, later, emerging from the back of a police patrol car at his five-star hotel, he was covered in vomit and other noxious substances. If that was not bad enough, his arrival coincided with the end of one of Stockholm's most fashionable balls. As Ian entered the lobby he met the cream of Swedish society dressed to the nines making their way home. The trick was to try to pass himself off as naturally as possible whilst elegant ladies and gentlemen turned their noses up and looked the other way.

Other books...

In the 1980s Ian spent time photographing vineyards and their owners around the world, on assignment with *Hologramme* to produce a book called *Women in Wine*. What amused Ian (and spoke to variations in a country's approach to wine making) was that a woman winemaker in California had given Ian exactly one hour whereas one of the women at an Italian vineyard was happy to spread the session over three days.

Ian was also offered an assignment to work on a book detailing the *30 Best French Restaurants*. Magnum photographers are not known for their work on food and restaurants. In this particular case, the original photographer had walked out in disgust halfway through (for whatever reason, Ian has never revealed). Ian, however, completed the project. Then, knowing his wife (a food journalist) would love the assignment, he agreed to produce the *30 Best Italian Restaurants*. Following this it was the *30 Best Spanish Restaurants,* gaining a stone in weight for each book.

Water, its use and abuse and the way it runs like a silken thread through all our lives, has fascinated Ian for many years. Anyone with an eye on the way the world's climate is changing and how fast the global population is growing will understand the problems the world will face soon, especially concerning fresh water. We have already touched upon this earlier in the book. Suffice to say it remains an issue Ian feels strongly about, and continues to explore as and when possible.

Talking with other photographers, it is clear that each one invariably develops a project (or projects), allowing them not only to pursue a theme of their own choosing but it provides them with different experiences, ones that they can follow in their own way. Ian's fellow Magnum photographer, Stuart Franklin, follows his interest in the British shoreline and produced a book based around that particular project. Ian's long-term project on water has come to maturity with the 2023 publication of his book: *Water* (Gost Books, London June 2023).

Developing an Ian Berry Style...

When Ian is shooting a story he endeavours to provide the client with images that meet their needs. This does not mean he will compromise his photographic integrity. Whatever happens Ian's intention is to remain true to how he sees the story.

Always the professional, Ian's patience was once tested a little by the editors of the *National Geographic* book division over a shoot entitled Discovering Britain and Ireland. One of the images he submitted was of an expanse of Hadrian's Wall, that stone border built by the Romans, stretching from the River Tyne in the East, over the Pennine spine, following the exposed Win Sill, to the Solway Firth and Cumbria in the West. It was only after the film had been processed and submitted, that Ian was contacted by the picture editors at the *National Geographic* with a request to reshoot the Hadrian's Wall picture. Initially, Ian had been pleased with that particular shot, and rightly so for it included two hikers in just the right spot to add something to the final image of the wall as it snaked its majestic way over the landscape. A patient man, Ian had seized upon the fortuitous appearance of these two hikers.

The trouble, as far as the picture editors were concerned, was that the two men were wearing dull jackets. The jackets had to be red! For those of us who love the paintings of Constable (and others), we are aware that the great master invariably added a small splash of red, be it a child's jacket or a piece of horse harness, to 'lift' his paintings. It was his way of adding an extra, dynamic element.

Obviously, the picture editor at *National Geographic* had decided to follow Constable's example.

This request came to Ian when he was back in London. To meet the brief, it would mean having to drive all the way from London to Housesteads (an archeological site on the Wall), a journey of close to 10 hours, for a single shot and then he would have to drive all the way back. Unfazed, he made sure he had a couple of similar looking hikers with him, and a couple of red jackets stowed in the boot of the car.

Jean-Marie Le Pen...

This commission had all the makings of a potential comedy (or a tragedy), yet it was a job that could prove 'interesting'. The request for the story came from the French magazine *Paris Match*. Ian was asked to photograph the French National Front leader Jean-Marie Le Pen. This was in 1986, at a time when the far-right nationalists were beginning to flex their electoral muscles and offer a jingoistic alternative to mainstream politics. Ian was famous for his work in South Africa and the Congo, especially as a photographer for the black African magazine *Drum*. The commissioning editors at *Paris Match* may have put two and two together and come to the conclusion that the famous Ian Berry must surely be black! Ah, how unfortunate for them that Ian, the Hampstead liberal, was white. What transpired, Ian says, was a good photoshoot. There is Jean-Marie, with whom Ian built an amicable relationship, sat with his dogs on the front steps of his house. It may not have pleased the *Paris Match* editor but it was a recognisably Ian Berry image.

Speed (cars and motorbikes)...

It is incongruous when you know Ian, this epitome of genteel Englishness, to imagine him in leathers, riding a very powerful motorbike, but this is all part and parcel of who he is. Jürgen Schadeburg remembers meeting Ian back in South Africa and noting his silk scarf and Triumph sports car. Yet, as you follow the story of Ian's life, there has always been a thread of speed running through it. Whilst a child in Lancashire, Ian's father had raced cars and later, in South Africa, Ian had taken to racing with his Triumph. If anything, it was the Triumph that made him decide to dedicate more of his life to photography. The cost of weekend racing in South Africa was exorbitant. The tyres alone were costing him a small fortune and the amount of oil the car used meant frequent fillings. That was until he fitted an aeroplane's oil filter. Besides, he never seemed to win much. It was the combination of these factors that led to Ian giving himself a talking to. The outcome of this interior monologue was to abandon the racing and concentrate instead upon the photography.

Sunderland, England
Two old ladies live together in a spotlessly clean small house

Hong Kong
A little old man bowed with years of hard labour emerges from the Mass Transit Railway (MTR) station with young office workers

Ian had ridden bikes since he was 14, taking his test on his 16th birthday. As the years went by the bikes grew both in size and in power, as each new one was bought. When Ian was vice-president of Magnum, he discovered that riding his motorbike was quicker than flying to Paris. On these occasions his bike was chained to the railings outside the office and next door to the police station, which had a constant presence of a gendarme visible at all times. Gendarmes, it should be remembered are armed at all times. Regrettably, on one occasion, Ian returned from lunch after being away for only an hour only to find the bike gone. Even the ever-present gendarme had not prevented the theft. Whoever had stolen the bike also took the chain.

Though Ian had lost his bike it was on a later occasion that the French police were very helpful. Ian came off his Norton Commando after a tank-slapper. This is when the bike's handlebars oscillate wildly with the inevitable result... bike and rider part company. The police took Ian to hospital, collected his bike and secured it in a police lockup.

Motorbikes have cropped up consistently over the years. When on assignment in Argentina in 1998, Ian, not being a horseman, chose to follow the gauchos on an off-road bike. *"It was the only way,"* he says.

When photographing the Vietnam War with his friend and fellow Magnum photographer, who died in 2018 Abbas, they decided to abandon the customary free access every journalist had to space on any convenient US Army helicopter. Instead they chose to use a jeep. If the intention was to exchange the very vulnerable helicopter for a less exposed mode of transport, this proved a fallacy. The jeep also proved unsatisfactory and was duly abandoned in favour of a motorbike. On this conveyance the two Magnum photographers tried to get to the front, Ian driving with Abbas behind, keeping the cameras dry.

Speed is still an element in Ian's life. Even as late as 2016, Ian owned a Seeley-Honda bike which he kept dry and safe covered by an American Army poncho he had bought whilst in Vietnam.

Vehicular transport has been important throughout Ian's life. What with the Land Rover he took to Africa, the powerful Jeep he was driving when I first met him, along with the many and varied motors he has had in-between, his experiences with motor transport could fill a book on its own. Imagine then, his delight should a vehicular-related assignments come his way. One such was the story he was assigned to work on photographing the Morgan Motor Company with its wonderfully anachronistic hand- built techniques. This could well have been Ian's equivalent to a pilgrimage.

Sometimes, though, the choice of car might not be appropriate. During the story of French vineyards Ian arrived at the Chateau Mouton Rothschild in a lowly *Simca*. Perhaps not the most fashionable of vehicles to park in front of such a venue. However, the Rothschilds seemed not to mind. As it transpired, the shoot went very well and the week Ian spent at the chateau was very pleasurable. Having just arrived from South Africa, Ian had not had time to accustom himself to the joys and subtleties of French wines. Sitting down to dinner became a daunting prospect as he was faced with three or four different wines to be served though the meal. Never sure which one to drink and which to leave, Ian chose not to offend his hosts and drank the lot.

Having "expensive" tastes...

One of the rewards from the Rothschild shoot was a case of a dozen bottles of very expensive wine, not that Ian was aware of the wine's value at the time as it was being loaded into the back of the *Simca*. The case of wine had been loaded along with his suitcase by the butler and Ian was unaware of its presence. Once it was packed and goodbyes said, Ian drove off oblivious of the treasure in the boot of the car.

At this time Ian was sharing a flat in Paris with one of NBC's cameramen, Ray Wilson. How civilised it must have seemed, to have this crate of Chateau Rothschilds finest to share with a friend whilst eating their somewhat frugal meals, *"usually beans"*. It was only when Ian arrived at a dinner party with the obligatory couple of bottles of wine for the hosts that he was made aware of just what they had been drinking. Though shocked, Ian tells me the party was a success and went with a swing! With vintage Rothschild wine, that is hardly surprising.

"When you're with me you order..."

There was a time when money in the corporate world was plentiful, and for photographers there were assignments to enjoy, curtesy of someone else's expense account. There are still the occasional ones out there, but the climate has changed. These free-spending corporations, with their global reach and fingers in many pies and in many countries, became bread and butter for reliable, professional photographers like Ian. It meant, however, being sent anywhere to photograph just about anything.

Some companies needed images for their annual reports (as with Hitachi and Reuters) whilst others sought to illustrate their work or to advertise their products. Working on a story for a company like the Italian coffee supplier Lavazza, meant a venue that emphasised the high end nature of the product. That would probably take Ian to somewhere like Istanbul. Other stories might require Ian to base himself in a tin shack in the middle of nowhere, with only rudimentary facilities.

One of the clients Ian has worked for several times is a manufacturer of a famous carbonated drink, one of those brands everyone recognises anywhere in the world. After several international commissions for the company in some of the most salubrious settings, Ian was embarrassed by one particular incident in Thailand. The conditions were comfortable and the company designer assigned to be with him was friendly enough. From the photographer's point of view they can (and often do) provide invaluable support and open many doors.

However, they can, at times, feel the need to interfere. It may come as a surprise to some to note that the agendas of executive and photographer may not be the same all the time.

As the shoot in Thailand progressed, Ian and the designer found themselves travelling along one of Thailand's many rivers in a small river boat. Nearing their hotel Ian noticed a saffron-robed Buddhist monk drinking a bottle of Pepsi. He was standing on the shore, in front of a temple. That, said Ian ironically, would make a great shot.

Early next morning, the designer woke Ian telling him he has arranged for the monk to be at the temple. Grabbing this gear, Ian followed. Arriving at the temple site, it was not one monk but a temple full of monks who waited patiently. Checking his cameras, Ian was further distracted when several crates of Pepsi were delivered and the monks smiled, then helped themselves. The shoot went ahead and Ian took his photographs whilst the monks slowly and continuously consumed bottle after bottle of the drink. The shoot turned out to be a great success. With sufficient images "in the can", Ian said he had finished. With that, the monks slowly merged back into the surrounding vegetation as if they had never been there, taking with them the rest of the bottles. Ian was left standing amidst the remnants of the shoot, feeling embarrassed at having participated in a horrible commercial shoot.

On a similar shoot for this company, and the day's work finished, Ian thoughtlessly asked for bottle of a rival's beverage. It was not meant as a slight. He was merely using a generic term for this particular type of drink but the executive took exception and, turning to Ian said, with a certain edge to his voice:

"When you're you're working for Pepsi, you will drink Pepsi."

Good fortune and the growth in shared assignments...

As costs rise and money for assignments shrink, those which can be sponsored by two or more bodies are becoming more the norm. His recent trip to Columbia is a case in point. One part of the assignment was to record the current situation of a country disrupted for many years by the FARC insurgency and the power of the various criminal drug-producing groups. Whilst the FARC rebels agreed a treaty in 2016 this was not the case with the drug gangs. One of Ian's assignments was to produce a story about Colombia in the early months of 2018. That was commissioned by the *Observer* magazine. Coupled with this was an assignment funded by Fair Trade, who wished to have a story on the production and distribution of their bananas.

This "clustering" had been a technique that Ian and many other photographers have employed before. In 1989, Ian worked on a story in Peru for *The Telegraph Magazine* where he photographed the smallest British Embassy in the world (which is situated in La Paz). Whilst there Ian was to cover the presidential campaign of author and Nobel Prize winner Mario Vargas Llosa. Ian's stay in La Paz evolved into a third story. He heard about a woman who worked with orphans. Ian photographed the story which was subsequently used in the *Telegraph Magazine*.

It was in 1958, when Goulden was travelling through the country, that she came upon an abandoned child. The boy was suffering from tuberculosis and meningitis which explains why he had been left to fend for himself. From then on, until her death in 2002, Goulden sought to provide all the help and support needed to care for these abandoned and handicapped children. Goulden was essentially broke and couldn't continue to pay the rent on the house she used as an orphanage. As a result of the *Telegraph* story, she received enough money in donations to enable her to buy the house and continue with her work. This was one of those occasions when a photographer was in the a position to make a difference and see an immediate benefit from their story.

Demonstrations and their attraction...

Back when Ian "was young and easy under the apple bough," he was no stranger to street demonstrations. This is not to say he enjoyed the violence, but the various small details of any protest make for interesting photographs. If you need confirmation of this just look at his images made during the American Embassy demonstration in London in 1968. Each frame shows how close he could get to the action and how tightly he composed a shot. One of Magnum's original creeds was that to crop an image was anathema to the photographer's professional sensibilities.

Ian's interest in the voices of the disenchanted has ranged from demonstrations by French farmers in Paris in 1992, to the anti-President Milosevic demonstrations around Belgrade in 1996, to the 1997 Oxford protests when the police were confronted by the *Reclaim the Streets* demonstrators. The year previous, Ian had been with the tree- squatters during the anti-Newbury By-Pass protests, and was there when the police arrived to remove the protesters.

In 2002, Ian was once again in Trafalgar Square covering the peaceful (and colourful) demonstration by the Sikh community as they declared themselves to be British and Proud. A year later, in 2003, he was back there photographing a peaceful May Day Protest Parade.

Another protest covered by Ian was that in Madhya Pradesh (India) when local people protested about the building of the Narmada Dam. Once again he was using colour film and, looking at the photographs from that story, it is easy to see why Ian found it best to use colour. There are many evocative images, including one of a smiling woman sheltering from the monsoon rain under a plastic sheet. These images are, in their own way not only colourful but are generous in their intention and respectful in the way they portray the subjects. Other protesting villagers shelter beneath a collection of rain soaked dark umbrellas, but, once again Ian's eye founds a single splash of colour, a saffron scarf, amidst the monotones. The colour of saffron is invariably vivid and occurs in other images from that protest. A flotilla of fishing boats cast off as part of the demonstration, leaving behind a single woman, dressed in her saffron-coloured sari.

Should anyone be tempted to suggest Ian produces a book of world-wide protests, he has sufficient "copy" to produce a, if not **the**, definitive photobook. His travels have brought him into 60 years' worth of contact with protests and protestors. I have often wondered why Ian is drawn to these type of incidents. Was it a simple urge to be there? Does the adrenalin kick in? No, if anything, Ian is the least likely journalist to respond to his own adrenalin surge. If this were the case then he would have been drawn to *The Bang-Bang Club* in South Africa, when he was there covering the inter-tribal violence, as were others who willingly became members of *the club*. But their approach is not one he finds useful, or even palatable. It ignores the wider picture, and by so doing does not tell the whole story. Many of those who were involved in the upheaval in some way, usually to a lesser extent, were ignored.

The Bang-Bang Club was the name given to a group of four photojournalists who came to prominence during the South African troubles of 1990 to 1994. Kevin Carter, Greg Marinovich, Ken Oosterbroek and João Silva were drawn to photographing the violence and the results of the violence. A book was later published by Marinovich and Silva called The *Bang-Bang Club* which was turned into a film of the same name in 2011.

Whilst the *Bang-Bang Club* sought out the dead and dying Ian gave a voice to those who remained on the sidelines and, you could argue, were equally victims and dispossessed.

Ian suffers from a much older condition. Like many of his contemporaries, he has a sense of **duty**. In a way, he feels privileged to be following a calling that is both his hobby and his livelihood, and if there is a story to be told and that story happens to be one a wider audience need to share in, then it's his job to make sure the reporting is as honest and as balanced as possible. Photographers like Ian can only photograph what is there to be photographed and the presenting of honest images is part of their professional job description. Unlike an art photographer, there can be none of the photographer's personality or values advising a photographic record of an event. Whatever the subject, the images must be trusted.

His insatiable curiosity has led Ian to return to South Africa many times, especially to record the aftermath of the radical changes wrought by the end of apartheid's National Party Government. Once again, Ian was covering dissension and conflict and those facing acts of unacceptable violence. Witnessing the killing of perceived traitors by the placing of tyres over the body, restricting the movement of the arms, pouring petrol over the victim and then setting light to the person was one of the horrors that came from the hatred and frustration of those who felt they had no other way of finding justice. Archbishop Desmond Tutu hated the practice and threatened to take his family and leave South Africa for good. Others said the practice worked and made potential police spies think twice about betraying their fellow township citizens. All this Ian witnessed.

Armenia...

In 1993, Ian went to Armenia for *The Independent* magazine on a story about Leninakan five years after the earthquake. It was winter, as it had been back in 1988 when the earthquake struck the area near to the city of Spitak. December 7th, in the morning, an earthquake registering a surface wave magnitude of 6.8 hit the region and lasted for less than 20 seconds. In that time it was estimated between 25,000 and 50,000 people were killed (there was a further estimate in 2017 that calculated the death toll was 38,000) and a further 130,000 were injured.

One of the problems the engineers and rescue teams faced was the unstable conditions of the remaining buildings. The Metsamor Nuclear Power Plant, though suffering only minor shaking, was closed for six years due to concerns about its vulnerability. The shoddy workmanship and devastation was publicly blamed on concrete that had been used in the construction of many of the buildings. *Pravda* claimed it had been adulterated during the Era of Stagnation (also known as the Brezhnevian Stagnation), when concrete was a source of additional income and had been stolen in large amounts.

The Russians had promised to rebuild the city and, true to their word, they had started. For whatever reason the work had been abandoned. Ian found a city of half-finished buildings and acres of abandoned equipment: rusting cranes, earthmover and other large items of construction machinery. It was the middle of winter and there was only one new building able to function and that was the hospital, still treating people for the injuries they sustained during the earthquake. Many of the other residents who remained in Leninakan were forced to live in old railway coaches and sea containers.

With no hotel, Ian was invited to stay with a kindly family in their freezing sea container. The rebuilding had stopped before any shops could be built and Ian spent a couple of days walking the streets without anything to eat. It was the generosity of ordinary people who fed him from their meagre supply of food, a supply they could ill afford to share. There were no public places to eat but the people were *"terrific"* and went out of their way to provide Ian with something to eat. These offerings seemed to be mainly tins of peaches. As with the people in Prague, Ian was acutely aware that these offerings were precious and was loath to accept. The dilemma being any refusal on his part could be seen by those making the offer as an insult.

Walking the streets of Leninakan was dangerous for another reason. Ian was harassed by packs of feral dogs. Left to roam free and fend for themselves the dogs had reverted to wild behaviour. He was attacked and bitten several times. During one attack a dog took a bite out of Ian's leg. Fortunately, he was wearing a pair of Swedish leather boots which came high up his leg.

Ian had then to go to Azerbaijan on assignment. There were no flights. The hospital in Leninakan was supported by donations and the Red Crescent had ambulances criss-crossing Georgia. This seemed the only logical way out of Armenia and it was agreed Ian could travel in one of the vehicles on the way to Baku, Azerbaijan's capital.

Travelling north to Tbilisi, Ian spotted queues of people waiting outside a small bakery. There were too many people for Ian to push through to get to the bakery itself. However, just around the corner he spotted a van delivering bread down a chute. Following the loaves Ian arrived inside the bakery itself and was able to photograph the faces of the people in the queue.

Crossing eastern Georgia, there were wrecked lorries by the side of the road. Ian put these wrecks down to the harsh conditions of the road itself. Not so. His Red Crescent driver explained these lorries had been looted by bandits and left, abandoned along the road, to rot.

Azerbaijan had regained its independence after the collapse of the Soviet Union in 1991. Nevertheless, there was only just one functioning hotel in Baku, allegedly full of oil workers from all over the world. Fortunately, the Red Crescent driver knew a back door, guarded by an old Russian concierge who, for a backhander, found Ian a room. Today, the situation is very different and Baku is a beautiful, modern city with many world class hotels.

Azerbaijan and the Baku oilfields...

The assignment was for *Fortune* magazine and Ian was to visit the oilfields. *"The area was very polluted. You could taste the crude oil in the back of your throat."*

Accessing his accommodation and the place where he was to photograph meant Ian needed to be driven along roads that were lined by acres of barren ground covered with hundreds of *nodding donkeys pumps.* To a photographer like Ian all this was, perversely, a delight to photograph. To the outsider (or non-photographer), it may look like hell on earth but the various scenes, the characters and the general muck were a pleasure to shoot for any photojournalist.

Not being an Azerbaijani speaker and in need of transport, Ian required both a driver and an interpreter. The all-in-one "provided" for him would, it was hoped, be able to fulfil both roles. He turned out to be a police officer and Ian is still convinced the man was assigned to keep an eye on him. The vehicle this cop drove was an elderly Lada of questionable reliability. There is nothing Ian wishes to say that might be seen as detrimental to any Lada-owner in particular, or Lada in general. The vehicles are, for the most part, valiant and hard-working. However, this particular Lada had only three of its four forward gears working. When it came to a hill, getting up it was more an act of faith, wishful thinking (and post-Soviet prayers) than the effective functioning of the vehicle's mechanics. Once the brow of the hill was reached, both Ian and the driver could relax for a while, as the Lada would freewheel down the other side.

However, the story also called for aerial shots. After making his application to visit one of the offshore oil rigs, Ian was granted permission to fly there on one of the servicing helicopters which made regular trips to and fro. As is the common practice in such cases, this trip in a helicopter would involve a degree of risk. Ian had been on assignment for British Gas and flown to a North Sea rig and that had necessitated a series of health and safety rules. It also involved crashes but we have already mentioned those. With this experience behind him, Ian still expected to be given some sort of induction, a survival suit perhaps or, maybe, a brief explanation of how to use a life jacket and, possibly, how to cope should the helicopter ditch. No. Instead he was told to wait in a queue until the helicopter was ready to load, and then get on.

Ian joined the queue.

The helicopter landed and its door opened to disgorge a seemingly endless stream of returning workers. Just as he was about to embark, Ian was overtaken by a tsunami of workers to whom the idea of queueing was an unknown concept. Everyone rushed for the open door and fought to get on. Once the passenger compartment was full, anyone with a foothold on the helicopter was either pushed in or turfed off and the door slammed shut. The helicopter, fully laden, then departed.

Now, Ian found himself at the head of the queue but when the helicopter returned for a second load the same thing happened, leaving Ian battered, once again having been crushed by the rush.

If you can't beat them then join them! Therefore, the next time the helicopter landed, Ian joined the rush and fought his way on board. This was when he discovered that the only available space for him was standing, jammed up against the bulkhead. How was he to get his pictures? He asked the pilot if there was any provision for him to make his aerial shots. The pilot said that, "Yes!" There was. It was simple, *"You open the window!"*

This was not the only story Ian was involved in that necessitated visiting Baku. Three Magnum photographers were commissioned by an Italian oil company to record the laying of a pipeline under the Caspian Sea. The company was part of the AGIP group and the other photographers were Magnum colleagues. These two were also photographers whom Ian has great respect for: Steve McCurry and Alex Webb. According to Ian it was a good shoot and, best of all, the Italian company provided great food.

Hollywoodland...

From its inception, Magnum Photos has had a symbiotic relationship between its photographers and the film industry. Robert Capa had been in an intense relationship with the Swedish film star Ingrid Bergman which allowed access to film sets. From this grew other collaborations. Eve Arnold had photographed many film sets including the 1966 film *A Man for All Seasons,* Isabella Rossellini in Finland filming the *White Nights* and, perhaps Magnum's tour de force, *The Misfits*. Ian also photographed his fair share of films: the Paris street locations of the 1972 Fred Zinnemann film *Day of the Jackal*; the Yul Brynner film *Flight from Ashiya* (1962) and, in a more domestic situation, the 2016 General Election film made by Ken Loach for the Labour Party.

Ian was in the Rome studio of Cinecitta photographing the adventure/rescue film *Flight from Ashiya*. It starred Yul Brynner amongst others. Brynner was a keen photographer who enjoyed the company of fellow photographers. Scenes were being filmed that necessitated using the large wave tank at the studio. This concerned a group of children adrift on a life raft, their boat having been caught in a storm. Whilst up a ladder, covering the action, Ian lost his cameras. They fell into the tank. Upon their retrieval it was clear they were useless. The only answer then was to send the pair of Leicas off to NewYork to be fixed. So Ian could complete the assignment, Brynner lent him two of his Nikons. Mutual respect goes a long way especially when it comes to photography and Ian became a favourite photographer for Brynner. Theirs was to be a lifelong friendship, though Brynner died in New York in 1985, aged 65.

Paris was another place where Ian and Brynner met. Brynner invited Ian to breakfast with him, at a very expensive hotel on the Place de la Concorde. The food was good and the company even better. Trouble only came when Brenner was called away and Ian was left with the bill. I asked him if Brynner ever repaid him? *"Oh, I made sure I didn't lose out. I claimed it on expenses,"* said Ian and I swear there was a twinkle n his eye.

The Silk Road

"If you are going to photograph women in Mashhad, make sure there isn't a mullah close by!"

Iranian police officer

A paragraph in *The Guardian* mentioning the newly opened rail link in Iran attracted Ian's attention, and gave him an idea: it would be possible to follow much of the ancient Silk Road by train. This attracted Ian's attention and gave him an idea. It could be an opportunity to photograph the journey as a major story.

Ian let the idea marinate for a while before he approached Magnum. The New York office, along with the *Condé Nast Traveller Magazine*, thought it a good idea. What Ian did not expect when Condé Nast's New York office agreed to using the story was the stipulation the shoot be in black and white. Joy of joys! Any photographer who enjoys using rolls of Kodak Tri-X or Ilford HP5 will relish the challenge of capturing the nuances and textures of such a trip in their beloved black and white. "*Their picture editor must have seen my work and thought it a good idea!"* Ian Berry recalls. However, Ian made sure he shot the journey on colour negative film which meant that when it came to the European edition the picture editor used colour.

So, with their bags packed and his wife, Kathie, suitably kitted out, the first stage of their mammoth journey began, to Istanbul. Istanbul would give Kathie a chance to spend time with friends and Ian a chance to do what he does best: take pictures.

Istanbul should have been a time for them to relax and get into the mind-set for the journey. There were no constraints on their time and the company was pleasurable. It would also provide a foundation for the images that Ian would make during the rest of the journey.

Of all the places in Istanbul to photograph, there was one in particular that Ian wished to visit. This was the covered market. A monstrous, age-old temple to Middle-Eastern trade and consumerism. This was a place where bartering was an art form. The site itself covered a large acreage. To Ian it offered many, many opportunities to photograph the varieties of Middle-Eastern commercialism. The faces of the traders and the goods on sale would provide good copy.

"Enormous market; great to shoot, but people are getting more 'agin' being photographed. Anyway, it was fine and afterwards we stopped outside to talk. Unbelievably, I put my bag down on a wall. I had three Leicas around my neck, one with a 28mm lens, another with a 35mm lens and the third with a 50 mm lens. In the bag was a Nikon fitted with a 200mm f4 and there was an 85mm lens on its own. Then this guy grabbed the bag and disappeared. I chased him and in the chase the Nikon and 200mm lens fell from the bag. Stopping to pick up the Nikon the guy got away with the bag and the 85mm. The Nikon body was okay but the lens had jammed! I didn't have the 85mm, so the longest lens I now had was the 50mm on the Leica.

"I spoke to the guy we were with, a businessman, and he said the only way was to send stuff out but it would take an age and wouldn't arrive in time. We were booked on the train and that was fixed, so I thought to myself: I'd spent most of my life shooting with three Leicas so, to hell with it! We're going.

Mashhad, Iran

Women wait to board a bus through the back door, separated from the men who board at the front. An impatient driver guns the engine which swamps the women in exhaust fumes

"We travelled through Turkey which was pleasant and without incident, apart from someone throwing a rock through the carriage window; it was probably just a passing gesture.

"We thought we would have trouble entering Iran but not at all. The Iranians couldn't have been nicer. The Iranian immigration guy wanted to practise his English. He complimented me on my wife's attire, a full black burka, and we were waved through. Whilst on the train we befriended a lady who invited us to stay with her at her home. That was great! Once away from the public gaze the family, including her daughters, were very western. Off came their burkas to reveal colourful silk dresses." Ian Berry

Arriving at Mashhad, in Iran, Ian was at a disadvantage: being both male and European. Kathie, on the other hand, dressed in her burka and wearing large, dark glasses was able to pass unnoticed amongst the populace. Kathie is a vivacious blonde and her eyes are Nordic blue, hence the sunglasses.

"In Mashhad I watched whilst a bus pulled up at a stop and the men got on through a door at the front whilst the women used a door at the back. Biding my time I waited until another bus turned up. The men got on quickly enough and sat at the front. The women, however, encumbered by billowing clothes, took longer. The driver and the men were obviously impatient and the driver revved the engine in an effort to speed them up. The trouble was that the exhaust was at the back, by the women's entrance.

"Clouds of dark smoke engulfed the women and virtually obliterated them. As it ebbed away the women fought to get on. There was no orderly queuing. I stood at the back watching a sight that reminded me of a family of penguins and waited. It is my experience that, in such a situation, there will be one woman who invariably turns round and looks back. Anyway, that one woman turns round and I took the picture. Fine! And then I stood back and looked around and saw this mullah watching me. It was one of those moments when the hairs on the back of your neck rise and tell you that discretion is the better part of valour! There was going to be a problem so I legged it!

"I'd only gone a couple of blocks and I thought 'God! You're getting old Berry! You're getting nervous about nothing.' That was when I felt a tap on my shoulder and, turning round, I came face to face with a policeman. Ian Berry

Ian was marched off to a police post where he was confronted by the mullah. After the conversation between the secular and the religious had run its course, the mullah was pacified somewhat by the officers, and left the post. It was then Ian's turn to face the police officers. Probably, not for the first time this police officer was called upon to remonstrate with a European. Once the lecture was over Ian was allowed to go free. However, the arresting officer had one last comment to make:

"If you are going to photograph women in Mashhad make sure there isn't a mullah around!" police officer

From Mashhad the journey moved on to Ashkabat, the capital of Turkmenistan. It was here that Ian, wandering the streets in search of suitable subjects, photographed an enormous portrait of the president. Looking for buildings of interest to photograph, Ian discovered one that was built in the local style and looked old. No sooner had he focused his lens on the building's facade than he was approached by several men of bodyguard-like dimensions. Escorted inside, and fearing the worst, Ian discovered that he had inadvertently photographed the local headquarters of the FSB, the successor to the KGB. By then an expert in optimism and faith in his ability to talk his way out of dangerous situations, Ian managed to extricate himself and enjoy the inevitable coffee. This time the beverage was of a reasonable quality, though not up to Italian prison standards. It was at this point that one of the senior police men asked Ian if it was the same in Britain: were you allowed to photograph Scotland Yard? Back then it was still possible and Ian told him "Yes". Now that the situation has changed Ian is not so sure.

From Ashkabat, the route moved on to Uzbekistan and the capital, Tashkent. The market place, with its local colour, was an ideal place for travellers to visit (and photograph). Ian moved silently and slowly amongst the traders. Yet another man, dressed in civilian clothes, approached him and threatened Ian with arrest. This time, some sixth sense warned Ian that the civilian might be trying it on. Turning to the man and growling "bugger off!" Ian then returned to making his pictures. This chancer followed Ian for half an hour before finally giving up.

From Tashkent the next stage of the journey meant travelling across the Uzbek border into Kazakstan. Once more, the border crossing was trouble free. Kazakstan was somewhat of an anticlimax. No one wanted to arrest Ian!

However, moving into China proved to be a slow process. Up to that point the gauge of the various railways had remained constant. China's railways, on the other hand, ran on a different gauge. This required the carriages to be jacked up and loaded onto a framework with the appropriate bogie and wheelbase sizes. All this took the best part of a day.

For Ian and Kathie, Northern China was eye-opening. This is a predominantly Muslim area and continues to be perceived as a problem for the Central Government in far off Beijing. It is an area where the Han Chinese police patrol in groups of five or more, for mutual protection.

It was here that Kathie and Ian visited a Buddhist town and where Ian took his favourite shot of the journey: the young boy in his vivid monk's robes seemingly pretending to be Superman, though it was probably a mere adjustment of his clothing.

After the seven weeks' travelling on the train Kathie and Ian finally arrived in Xian. It was from here that they flew on to Beijing. Throughout the journey Ian had used colour negative film and provided *Condé Nast Travel* with enough images to devote a healthy eight pages to the magazine article. True to their word, the US edition was printed in black and white. When the magazine hit the European newsstands, the eight pages were all printed in colour.

The Camorra of Naples

One of the highlights of 1997 was a story on the Camorra, a mafia-like gang that flourishes in and around Naples. The Camorra is one of the oldest secret societies in Italy and is similar in many ways to the Mafia. Based in the poorer districts of Naples, the Camorra does differ from the Mafia in having a more horizontal organisational structure. This results in individual clans being able to act independently. It also means, however, that they are more prone to feud amongst themselves. Naples is one of the only two places in the world where Ian felt it necessary to hire a man to walk behind him carrying a gun.

Ian's images are in colour, which suits the various locations perfectly. Dominating the street scenes are the scooters. Men in white shirts eschewing the use of helmets and any other form of protection are photographed riding around, like cavaliers of old on their horses, each one showing off. Amongst Ian's photographs there are some groups of scooterists talking to other scooterists. There is even a shot of two young, blonde girls having their papers checked by two motorcycle police officers. However, it transpires that the scooter was or is the preferred way for the young criminals to rob the unsuspected in the streets, a phenomena that has since been exported to other cities around the world.

These gangs are rooted in the culture of the region, and have been for generations. It was whilst gathering his information that Ian heard that several gang members had been arrested and were being held in the local prison. Ian, intent upon photographing the building where these Camorra members were incarcerated, made his way there, only to be arrested. As on so many occasions before (and since), Ian explained his presence and his activities in such a way that he was believed. Perhaps it should come as no surprise that, whilst inside, he was treated to coffee, the like of which he had not tasted before and has not tasted since. *"It was the best!"*

Fin de siecle

As the 20th century drew to a close, Ian was as busy as ever. His globetrotting took him on assignments to Thailand, Malaysia, the Philippines and Singapore (from where he travelled on to Hong Kong and Manila). He worked for France Telecom photographing the Dordogne and Correze, Manche and Calvados which were all stories in sharp contrast to the one he completed on the Spitalfields Dog Show and the 53rd annual Grimaldi clowns' church service at Holy Trinity Church, Dalston (this taking place annually on 14th December).

I asked Ian if there was a highlight assignment for those last years of the 20th century. He thought for a while then explained about a double assignment where two stories were combined into one trip. This was a trip to India where he went to photograph a story about the Adivasis, the original inhabitants of India who were to lose their homes when the Narmada dam was completed. This visit was combined with a portrait session with Arundhati Roy, author and winner of the Man Booker Prize for Fiction for her novel *The God of Small Things.*

Access to Ms Roy was complicated by the fact that she was heavily committed to supporting the protests against the building of the Narmada dam. This did not deter Ian and his photographs show the protests. Ms Roy was, when Ian photographed her, a vivacious young lady of 35 and there she is beguiling the other protesters with her words and presence. Those conditions were ideal for Ian. The context was very colourful and his subject was so heavily involved in her activities, which meant she ignored the camera. As with other, similar, shoots Ian was happy with the natural narrative look of his work.

The telling of a story in pictures is a key motivator in Ian's work. In an earlier life he might well have been a monkish figure illustrating manuscripts (though the solitude of a monk's life along with the absence of people might not be to his taste), or he might have sat by a winter's peat fire in some Viking long house retelling a story from one of the Sagas.

The 21st century

With the new century came new assignments. British Gas continued to call upon Ian's services and sent him once more to the Philippines and thence to Kazakhstan. There were assignments in the USA. In 1992, Ian had covered the Boston campaign of the presidential hopeful, Ross Perot. In 2000, he was back in Boston for the building of a bridge. In keeping with his love of shapes and the dynamic of line, Ian has a liking for any construction that where a complexity of metal girders and colourful bits and pieces provide him with an interesting image.

Perhaps one of the most compelling examples of Ian's affinity with bridges is his photo story of that marvel of modern engineering and design, the Millau Viaduct in France. This sweeping and elegant cable-stay structure traverses the Gorge Valley of the river Tarn. The design chosen by the committee for the bridge was the joint submission by the British architect Sir Norman Foster and the French structural engineer Dr Michel Virlogeux. Construction started in October 2001. When it was just about completed, on 14th December 2004, Ian was there to photograph the final stages of its construction.

Manchester

Cities are undoubtedly one of Ian's happy hunting grounds. An inveterate traveller he is happy to wander alone amongst the streets and back alleys. Should anyone with a few days to fill and in need of a project, one that springs to mind is trying to work out how many miles Ian has walked and what percentage of his time he has invested in pounding the pavements of those towns and cities where he has photographed. It will be considerable. He claims that photography in a city is one of the best things to do. It doesn't have to be a capital city in an exotic foreign country. As if to emphasis this Ian points to just one of the British cities he has photographed several times over the years... Manchester. As far back as 1966, when he attended the Labour Party Conference, he was there to photograph the film director Lindsay Anderson. He returned in 1968 with the popular songstress Dusty Springfield.

In 1997 it was the turn of Bolton to be the object of his lenses, and in 1998 he was back once more to photograph the activities of the youth in Salford and the Lowry Centre where Ian's photographs were subsequently exhibited. L. S. Lowry, a notable local artist as well as rent collector, is one of the most iconic British painters of the second half of the 20th century. His work has not only become highly collectable but is a record of the life and times of the industrial North West. It came as no surprise that his paintings were used by the Northern Ballet as the basis of their production of *A Simple Man*, which premiered on the BBC in 1987. Lowry's story is now a film (*Mrs Lowry and Son*, starring Venessa Redgrave and Timothy Spall) which was first shown at the Lowry Centre in 2019.

The mixture continues as before

Celebrating the anniversary of the Louisiana Purchase gave rise to frantic activity in the state. The purchase of 1803 brought a large tract of country into the newly independent United States of America. This purchase from France included more that just the southern state of Louisiana, it included most of what we now regard as the Mid-West reaching as far north as Montana on the Canadian border. Needless to say, the 200th anniversary celebrations provided a rich assemblage of scenes and stories. Moss-covered trees and antebellum mansions along with "southern belles" in period costume and stern-wheel paddle steamers on the Mississippi, the latter contributing to Ian's long-term water project.

On a more prosaic and domestic level, Ian was again involved in British politics when he covered the 2001 General Election. This time he accompanied the Labour Party's Peter Mandelson and the Conservatives' Michael Portillo as they travelled around the country, speaking at hustings and working hard to drum up support for their respective parties. These images could have been the stock pictures of the candidates as they paraded their public faces but, after so many years experience, Ian manages to capture more intimate moments, when these hardened politicians reveal the humanity that lies behind their well-practiced political carapace.

There are, sometimes, stories where life assumes a somewhat surreal aspect. Ian became involved in a book about South Korea. This involved several Magnum photographers and, as well as the book, there would be a major exhibition of the photographs. Amongst the other Magnum members working on the story was Ian's good friend Hiroji Kubota, whose hard work had instigated and guided the project.

One of the more bizarre events Ian photographed, though some may argue this was in keeping with Korean business practices, was the Mud Festival. This was (and still is) an excuse for shedding the formal restrictions of everyday (business) life and just having a good time.

A bizarre event taking place at the same time as the festival was a corporate bonding exercise for a group of bankers. This involved participation in a series of quasi-military manoeuvres in the estuary mud. The participants had not realised quite what was involved in these exercises and were completely covered in mud as well as being utterly exhausted.

This was in 2008 and now, ten years later, as Ian reflects upon the story he ends the telling of the tale by adding he ruined a perfectly good pair of shoes and a camera bag.

The Three Gorges Dam project

One of Ian's favourite countries to visit, and in which to photograph, is China. Though there can be restrictions, the people are friendly and accommodating. Ian puts this down to their respect for the elderly and venerable looking. *"Having white hair and a beard helps."*

One of the Chinese projects that became a major story for Ian was a journey down the Yangtze River and recording The Three Gorges Dam project. Construction had started in December 1994 and it opened for the generation of electricity in 2003. Work was carried out at a cost of US$31.765 billion, giving some idea of the immense size of the project. The reservoir it created covers an area of 419 square miles with a maximum length of 370 miles. From an ecological point of view, the electricity produced by the dam's generators is the equivalent to the annual burning of 84,000,000 tonnes of coal in an assortment of coal-fired power stations. For Ian, as you would expect, it was the way the dam had affected the lives of the people that he wanted to photograph. By 2008, China had relocated 1.24 million residents.

Getting to the site of the dam would cost Ian $5,000 for an official permit. That was unacceptably high and certainly not an amount he wished to spend. Instead, Ian hailed a taxi and asked to be taken to the dam. From there he took a local ferry. The cost of the taxi for the journey was $20. I thought it was just Yorkshire folk (like myself) who had to be forced to open their wallets but, then again, Ian has Scottish blood running somewhere in his veins.

With his benign "wise-old-man" looks, Ian made the most of the ferry ride and was able to photograph a great many intimate scenes along the river: the demolition of buildings in Wanxian for one; Sichuan fishermen struggling against the fast currents for another. One of his enduring images is that of a woman asleep next to her temporary home as she waits to be relocated before the area is flooded. Ian's photographs reveal the sadness of displaced people; whilst some are obviously scared as to what the future will bring them. For many it would be a move of 1,000 kilometres from their homes to Shanghai to live in a city where they didn't speak the language. Some merely look bemused and others seem resolved to make the most of the opportunities on offer. Ian's work, as you would expect, is very much about the effect of this project upon the lives of the people, rather than the physicality of the dam-building processes.

Near Yichang, Hubei Province, China
A woman sits in despair in the ruins of her home, demolished to make way for the Three Gorges Yangtze dam

Going digital

It was inevitable that Ian, long with just about every other photographer, changed from using film to "go digital". We can all mourn the demise of film, but the development of digital photography has brought a sea-change in the way a photographer works. Prior to 2005, Ian was a film and analogue camera devotee. His loyalty lay with the classic black and white film stock of Ilford and Kodak.

From 2005, however, he began to find using digital imagery was "*the way forward*". In 2006, nearly all his work was digital and in colour. The advantages of digital is that you can have many more images on a memory card and there isn't the need to load fresh rolls of film at critical moments during a session. One other benefit of digital is that you can photograph in colour knowing that it can be converted to mono in a matter of seconds on the computer, without losing the original.

The consequential development of photographic software such as Adobe Lightroom and Photoshop make manipulation so very easy. One disadvantage is that the mechanisms for saving the image can change over time thereby causing the photographer a problem should he or she wish to access an old file. Whatever happened to the floppy disk? Having asked that, it is no coincidence that the current methods of image storage have grown to the point where the complexities of the modern digital camera and their capacities are easily catered for.

Though Ian "claims" not to be technically minded, and even employs "an expert" to come and set up his systems he is, nevertheless, skilled when it comes to working on his Mac.

Santiago de Compostela, Galicia, Spain
A woman chef in the upstairs kitchen of a café in one of the narrow, paved streets off the main square, beats a mixture with a balloon whisk

Santiago de Compostela,
Galicia, Spain
Pilgrims who have walked the Santiago way arrive exhausted at an accommodation office near the cathedral

The elusive photographer

When I tried to contacting Ian early in 2013, I was told he was in Morocco. I tried again later only to discover he was in Rome working on a commercial project for Panasonic cameras. Time and again I tried to make contact only to discover that he was somewhere out there, in the world, taking pictures.

When it comes to getting this biography published, it became essential for Ian and myself to sit with the publisher and discuss how it might happen. Once again, telephoning him only ran up against the problem of trying to tie an internationally renowned Magnum photographer to a specific date when we three (Ian, Chris the publisher and me) could meet. Shakespeare's Three Witches had an easier time.

Ian's hectic schedule meant more time spent in France, and another trip to China (to Qingdao, a coastal city halfway between Beijing and Shanghai and one of those fast-growing conurbations with a current population of over 9 million and destined to grow even larger and faster). Compounding this, 2015 was also the anniversary of the signing of the Magna Carta. Living close to Salisbury, Ian had become heavily involved in the cathedral's celebrations. Salisbury has one of the original copies of the Charter. This led him to develop a project based upon King John and his actions during that momentous year of 1215. Ian travelled around the country creating a comprehensive collection of photographs telling the story from King John's meeting with the barons at Runnymede to his death after the disastrous crossing of the Wash.

Politics... again

As for our meetings, they were sandwiched between a plethora of photo assignments. For Ian, a golden opportunity to enter the cut and thrust of politics presented itself when David Cameron, then the prime minister, offered the country a referendum on membership of the European Union. Relishing the prospect of following some of the more colourful characters, Ian shadowed the Member of the European Parliament and staunch Brexiteer Nigel Farage. He was on hand to photograph the Conservative MP and minister Priti Patel, witnessing her being ejected, very politely, from Salisbury Cathedral's Close. Then he followed the leader of the Labour Party, Jeremy Corbyn MP, recording his contribution to the campaign.

The outcome of the Brexit referendum resulted in a decision to leave the European Union. Though the majority voted to leave, the margin was slight and caused considerable anger and disunity amongst the British population. This was especially true when the relationship between Northern Ireland and the Irish Republic was put into question. Into the mix came the Scottish National Party, which still favours an independent Scotland. Their dream of a Scottish nation was given credence by the large numbers who voted to remain in the European Union. Protesters gathered outside the Palace of Westminster lobbying various MPs as they entered and left the Houses of Parliament became a daily events. Not far away, the ghost-like figure of Ian Berry could be found capturing the vagaries of the various protesters.

Salisbury and the Cathedral

In 2017, Ian's close ties with Salisbury Cathedral meant that a large percentage of his work revolved around the various exhibitions of works by national and international artists. Ian's customary tact and quiet approach allowed him to work within the building and to become familiar with its nooks and crannies. Church of England cathedrals have their own ways of working with photographers. Some, like Durham, allow for none unless a fee is paid and a permit obtained, though this is changing to a more liberal and open policy. Others, like Newcastle upon Tyne have no restrictions at all. Salisbury falls within the two. What is common to the staff of every cathedral is their refusal to allow the use by photographers of tripods and flash guns. Ian possesses several tripods and flash guns along with other lighting gear but they are invariably superfluous. He can't remember when he last used any of them.

With his usual tact and quiet nature Ian, once more, exhibits his ghost-like approach to capturing the essence of an event, a place or the people involved. This time all expertise has resulted in photographs that show the grandeur and the beauty of the cathedral along with its intimacy and fine detail. This ability to become part of the background has meant he is able to photograph cathedral events sympathetically.

One of our more recent meeting happened the week or so before the *Novichok* attack on Sergei and Yulia Skripal. Needless to say, Ian was out and about recording the life and times of post-nerve agent Salisbury. What he found as he walked the streets of central Salisbury was a distinct lack of examples of panic-stricken people. If anything, the people of Salisbury were as sanguine as they always were, relaxed outside the various cafes should the sun be shining. On the plus side, he found parking a lot easier (and mostly free). If anything, it was the absence of the multitude of tourists eager to view the majestic 123-metre spire (one of international fame) of the cathedral and the lack of people on the streets, that spoke of the poisoning.

Sicily

Ian is a great reader filling empty hours whilst working on a story away from home with a thriller and or a whodunnit novel. It came as no surprise when he took advantage of a trip to Sicily to photograph the film sets for the *Inspector Montalbano* television dramas. Based upon the books by the author, Andrea Camilleri (very regrettably recently deceased), these stories are filmed in various locations. Montalbano's house is in Punta Secca whilst the harbour is the port of Donnalucata. Keeping the book firmly in mind Ian photographed many of the locations and, when appropriately, added to the story by covering the context in which the books are set. The end results were Sicilian images which range from the diablo-effect of Mount Etna's smoke cloud, to sunbathers on holiday, to police officers visiting a bar, to the market square in Catania and the flowers that thrive on the fertile ground close to Mount Etna.

Catania, Sicily

A market trader takes a drink from a tap in a brilliantly painted wall

London, England

In the midst of Brexit demonstrations outside the Houses of Parliament an apposite juxtaposition of the Brexit poster and one on a bus advertising a theatre show – 'Only Fools and Horses'

Considering in-depth coverage (Egypt as the example)

To produce a stand-alone travel book, you would need to have not only a great many images to select from but a wide range of subjects that would cover many aspects of the life and activities pertaining to that country. After many visits to Egypt, Ian would probably find he had no problem in provide a more than adequate range of suitable images. Placing to one side the shifting political climate, but wishing to understand the minutia of Egyptian life, he has covered everything from domino-playing young men to flat-bread sellers and camel-riding security guards (not to mention President Nasser *"on a fictitious camel by the pyramids"*).

Back in 2006, Ian was there photographing life on the Nile. Because of a motorcycle accident which resulted in a broken leg, a trip down the river was thought a good way to aiding his recovering. The warmth, coupled with being restricted in how much he could or needed to walk, plus the opportunity to add to his ongoing water project meant this was a win-win situation. Travelling in a leisurely fashion allowed Ian to concentrate upon the life lived by the side of the Nile. It was this trip that resulted in his photographing children working in the fields, and fishermen on a tributary of the Nile.

Though somewhat of a more prosaic nature, for another story Ian photographed the camel riders on the lookout for tourists and this provided a chance to photograph contrasting images of the slums which house the factory workers. British Gas were once again providers of opportunities to photograph stories on the gas rigs anchored off the coast.

Working on stories for international magazines, Ian would be in some of the famous historic sites, one of which was the Valley of the King, part of the ancient city of Thebes. Ian was working on a story that included this ancient site in 2008. In 2009, Ian was in the Sinai. It was here that he was covering a story about the effects of the weather upon the sandstone of buildings. Other stories from the same region will provide more evidence of how wide Ian's coverage can be. One of those stories was about camel racing that plays a central part in the lives of Bedouin tribesmen. In stark contrast, the other was one about St Catherine's Greek Orthodox Monastery.

Ian's kaleidoscopic view of Egyptian life would be incomplete without his record of life in and around Sharm-el-Sheikh. Distanced from the political machinations of life in the north, close to Cairo, Sharm-el-Sheikh is a holiday venue with all the rich variety such a destination offers: its luxurious and air conditioned shops; its five-star hotels and assorted facilities for wealthy tourists. Such a wealth of images provide a rare insight into a country most people now only know through news reports of violence, repression and archaeology. Ian's work meets his aim of providing as balanced a view of a place as possible. The truth lies in the detail.

The changing nature of Magnum

The dream of the founders of Magnum Photos was to establish a collective of photographers whose shared values were humanitarian, whose work would be controlled by the members of Magnum themselves and who would use the rewards of that work to support each other financially as well as emotionally and intellectually. Its early members were drawn from the top photojournalists of the day and this continued to be so for many years. When Ian presented his work to Henri Cartier-Bresson back in 1962 this was still the case.

Anyone who has knowledge of the nature of Magnum will know that it functions very much like a family. Its annual meeting can be an "interesting" affair with heated discussions about money and work. Money is a necessity when it comes to supporting photographers and paying staff at the various offices. What has changed though is the market place. This is a concern raised by many photographers, not only those in Magnum. There is a dearth of commissioned work. Cost, rolling news programmes on television, the demise of newsprint and the ubiquity of the smart phone have all contributed to the change of news gathering. Add to this the readily available of news (and opinion) constantly available on social media and the global ability to update information on computers and smartphones, this is hardly fertile ground for the photojournalist.

Out of the colleges and universities, each offering their own version of the multiplicity of photographic, media and design courses, come the young turks armed with their all-singing and all-dancing digital cameras. Each with a dream and keen to fight for a share of the marketplace.

While they may have the technical skills to work the camera, what they lack is a way of 'seeing'. something that only comes with a lifetime of experiences. It is more than just the gift of seeing a potential shot. It is more subtle in that it involves the ability to "know" what will make a good photograph and tell a story with grace and simplicity and the minimum of fuss. This is why the likes of Ian Berry are still sought out for stories that matter.

Appendices

Appendix I

Thoughts (and other matters)

At the end of every conversation with Ian there are always strands and bits that dangle like unfinished threads on a carpet. Giving these odds and ends a home is what this section is about. Mostly, these are quotes from Ian that offer you, the reader, a better insight into how Ian works and thinks. Some of these quotes refer to the use of film, which many photographers still favour, though Ian does use digital cameras mostly now.

With grateful thanks to Bryn Campbell, World Photography, Hamlyn publishing, London 1981.

"In photography, one tries to show what is happening and also to produce an exciting shape. One without the other is not enough. It is a question of balance, of making all the various elements work together."

"For me, the excitement is in the fraction of a second [when you take a picture]. It is an instinctive rather than an intellectual process."

"I like to think of myself as an observer and I work as inconspicuously as possible. I do not want to create or to influence the event I am photographing."

"The less one intrudes, the truer the picture."

"I never consciously shoot for a particular kind of market. Basically, I shoot for myself."

"Going on an assignment opens up new picture-taking situations."

"It is far easier to catch the feeling of a situation in black and white than in colour, which is more artificial in its effect."

Colour *"has been a limiting influence in my work, firstly, because there is an added risk of the eye being distracted from the main subject by a random splash of colour, and secondly because of the extra technical problems involved in shooting it."*

"In black and white you virtually never miss a picture for technical reasons. It is a far more tolerant medium in terms of exposure and, since you always have the same type of film in your camera, you are always ready to grab a picture if one offers itself."

"Since my style of working is essentially unobtrusive, I try to keep equipment to a minimum. I use 35mm cameras exclusively, with a mixture of Olympus SLRs and Leicas." Ian is now almost exclusively using Olympus digital cameras, form their lightness and convenience.

"With a 35mm lans I can compose and shoot very rapidly. With a 50mm lens it's a more considered lens. I use it in situations where I stand off and wait for the event to develop before I shoot. It's not a grab lens."

"When I walk around the streets I am looking for two things: I am watching for situations that may develop, and I am staying alert for situations that develop before I can think about them."

"I rather dislike very long lenses, partially because of the flattening perspective that usually results, and partially because they suggest a 'peeping tom' element. I don't like being caught pointing a long lens at somebody."

"Over 90% of the time I use available light."

Should it be necessary Ian takes along a few flashguns — *"If the only way to produce a picture is to rig up three or four flashguns, I'll do it. I think that I owe that much to the people who are paying me to be there."*
One of Ian's photo sessions with the scientist Stephen Hawkins required Ian to use flash and he is still dissatisfied with the results.

For colour film [back in the days when Ian had to shoot in film] — *"Usually, when the light is so abysmal that I cannot shoot with 400 ASA (ISO) Ektachrome then I use a tiny flashgun to open up the foreground."* One of the features of digital photography is that you can shoot easily enough in colour and then convert to black and white should there be a need.
(Taken from Bryn Campbell's wonderful book...)

Appendix II

The Technical Bits

"Its crazy that I'm buying [new] cameras at my age!" Ian Berry (2017)

Throughout his life Ian has experienced just about every marque of camera. Experience has taken him from large format *Linhof* plate cameras to the 120 roll film Rolleiflex and thence to a variety of 35mm film cameras: the Leica, the Contax and the Nikon, amongst others. Now Ian uses the smaller, mirror-less cameras that do just about everything but make the tea.

Whilst Philip Jones Griffiths was alive, Ian could rely upon him to offer sound, technical advice. *"Philip would say to me, have you tried such and such, and I would. The trouble, now, is that there is so much built-in obsolescence. No sooner have you developed one thing than another, bigger and better, comes along,"* Ian Berry explains.

Back in 2000, Ian was on an assignment for Magnum, to photograph the effects of a tsunami on a part of Bangladesh. This meant Ian arranging access to the spit of land which had suffered spectacular damage. With nothing but a track accessing this spit, a motorbike was the logical mode of transport. Once the shoot was done, Ian waited for the bike to come and pick him up. It failed to arrive with the result that Ian walked the six miles back to his accommodation lugging his heavyweight kit. It was then that he decided to "downsize".

Using the latest mirror-less cameras, such as the Panasonic and the Olympus, provides Ian with an excellent base upon which to build a collection of lightweight kit. There is one problem, however, and that is the demands these cameras place upon the batteries. Back in the day, when you could rely upon a Nikon battery to last you a couple of days, there was a need to carry just a couple of batteries and a single charger. The bulk of your gear back then would be the many rolls of film you needed to carry.

Now, the demands made upon the batteries mean you carry at least three for your day's use. With three cameras that means nine batteries all needing to be charged, usually overnight.

"In an assignment to Northern Ghana I had to stay in a doss house. The power supply was a single electric light bulb. With an adapter I could charge one battery at a time. The only way to charge them all was to keep waking up throughout the night to change the batteries."

Even suggesting a solar-run battery charger doesn't work. Most batteries need charging overnight ... when there is no sun!

One advantage of a digital memory card is that you can house a great many images on a small space. The downside is that they are easier to lose! Ian only carries 8gb SD cards. This means that should he misplace a card, not all the images will be lost. On one assignment Ian was "gathered up" by the local police. He was challenged to hand his card over to a belligerent official.

Being a resourceful chap Ian was able to palm his working card and hide it inside his shoe, giving him the chance to hand an unused card to the official. Fortunately, this official seemed not to have anything available whereby he could "read" the card. Ian was soon on his way.

There is another advantage to digital photography and that is the ability to review your work as you go along. Rolls of film need developing and this is usually best done away from the assignment, in clean and light-proof facilities, ones with an adequate supply of water. Whist in the Congo, during the civil wars that followed upon independence, the canisters of exposed film were usually transported to safety by a rota of fellow photojournalists who made the precarious journey through volatile territory that was invariably controlled by groups hostile to journalists, who they universally believed to be spies.

When on assignment now, Ian also carries a laptop which gives him access to his images and allows for a degree of editing. Unfortunately, the laptop also requires a battery and an appropriate charger.

"There is a lot to be said for not worrying about running out of film in the middle of a shoot. The question you would ask yourself was: 'Shall I change the film now? Shall I use up these last few frames etcetera and keep being professional?" Ian Berry

Wearing one of those ubiquitous sleeveless jackets all photographers seem to possess, Ian describes his routine: *"Fresh [cards] in this side and exposed ones in this side."* (Ian indicates which pocket he's referring to). Ian notes that I place masking tape over the battery terminals allowing me to keep charged batteries together. "And I have a little pack that keeps two batteries apart."

As for the modern design of cameras: *"I miss having F stops on the lens, having to go into the menu is laborious."* With the non-electronic film cameras, the limitation of having a roll of film with a fixed ISO meant that changes were achieved by adjusting the focal length and shutter speed. Experience meant that the distance could be estimated with accuracy and the speed and focal length altered as you approached the subject.

"Feeling less obtrusive with three Leicas, setting the ISO to 320 and the focal length at F2.8 you knew what your lenses would give you, especially the 28mm, 35mm and 50 mm. The trouble with autofocus, it can lead you astray. That's why I still prefer manual focusing." Ian Berry

Back in the 1970s the best lenses are prime lenses. It was Philip Jones Griffiths when in Cambodia who started to use a 70-200mm zoom. After buying a Canon along with a small zoom lens, Ian still felt it was too big. It was also obtrusive and he felt more comfortable with his three Leicas. They suited his way of working better.

Clothing is always an issue. Wax jackets were out of the question. The wax would, somehow, find its way onto the lens, there to cause problems. Try to remove the wax stains from a lens and you know what Ian means. Modern bad weather gear is great should you be a mountaineer or a trekker, especially when using breathable materials like *GoreTex*. However, these new, slippery fabrics can be far from ideal when the strap slips off your shoulder at an inopportune moment. There is an older fabric, *Ventile*, which is waterproof, has a matt finish and can be warm in cooler climes. It is a decent compromise but if you are working in a country like India, it is far too heavy. What does make sense, and an option Ian has used many times, is to resort to a large umbrella, which offers protection from the rain for both the photographer and the camera.

"I did have a Barbour jacket and was wearing it in Paris one day when I met Henri [Cartier-Bresson]*. I was doing an outdoor shoot. He saw my coat and asked what it was, so I told him. Next time we met he was wearing a Barbour jacket."* Ian Berry

Barbour jackets are produced on the banks of the River Tyne, originally to meet the taxing conditions experienced by North Sea fishermen. Now, with the company producing a wide selection of high-end clothing the company caters for a very wide customer base including foul-weather clothing that is not waxed.

Tripods are something Ian rarely uses. Having said that, he has six. Over time they have become smaller and lighter and this means that there are occasions when the smallest one might be packed, just in case. *"I like to be able to move with everything I have, including my camera bag."* Ian Berry

Ian will only use an exposure meter when he has film on the shoot. There are situations where modern cameras can be dangerous. Ian photographed several annual reports for British Gas. When you are in a refinery the demands of Health and Safety are paramount and anything that might cause a spark or ignite a flammable source is not allowed. This is a venue where anything that is analogue and battery-free can be essential. In those cases Ian would know in advance and use only a film Leica and/or a film Contax.

The Contax II was the first of the Contax 35mm camera Ian owned. It was a bit noisier than the Leica, having a metal shutter, but featured a quicker lens fit than the Leica. Leica used Ian to advertise their R4 and R5 cameras, both single lens reflex in design. When used in hot countries, Ian found that the R4 took pictures all by itself.

Asked how many rolls of film he might use, Ian said anything up to 100 rolls of film on a corporate shoot.

As for camera bags, Ian has three of different sizes. Packing as tightly as possible allows him to keep his equipment close when travelling by air. Small bags can, sometimes, be stashed under the seat.

"Coming back from Paris recently, I had my small rucksack on my shoulder. I was flying on a small Flybe aircraft to Southampton. Anyone with a fair sized wheelie was being stopped. These bags were being put into the luggage hold. My rucksack was stashed in the cabin locker and my small bag went under the seat."

A final word as to travel and practicalities: *"Customs can be a problem."* The variety that Ian has experienced could constitute a book on its own. Passing through Frankfurt all the kit was opened, yet Paris allowed Ian through without any fuss. Entering the USA does depend upon what the current policy may be. On arriving at the border control at one of the major US airports Ian passed through the X-ray portico only to find that one of the TSA ladies forced him to remove his specially purchased protective box, one designed to keep film safe from X-Rays. Ian had 120 rolls of exposed film and no amount of explanation could prevent the TAA needing to see every one of the 120 rolls. Only after the last one had been inspected was Ian allowed to repack his box and board the plane.

You could say that the value of a camera (especially one used by a famous photographer) depends upon the prevailing market conditions. Ian bought a Leica M2 from fellow Magnum photographer Eric Lessing for £35. Later, Ian traded it for £90 when he upgraded to a Leica M3. This camera was later sold at Christie's Auction House for £5,000, because of its provenance.

Appendix III

During a recent conversation with a Reuter's photographer I asked if he knew of the *Bang-Bang Club*. Yes, he did. Why? he asked. Until I started reading about South Africa and its history, especially the period that covered the years of apartheid and immediately afterward, I had only the vaguest idea of what life was like for the average South African. What didn't register in my brief overview is the importance of the tribal conflicts that have blighted the continent. It is far too easy to forget the diversity of people, even when considering a small geographic area. The innate differences between the Zulus of the Inkatha Party and the mainstream ANC sounds simple enough but they are far from simple. They are, in fact, very complex. This aspect of the conflict was documented by the *Bang-Bang Club*, a group of young white photographers who spent their time photographing this violent aspect of South Africa's story. It needed recording. It was, after all, an important part of the development of the Rainbow Nation.

What would my friend the Reuter's photographer have done? Pretty much the same he said. And this answer, the implicit acknowledgement that a photojournalist would be out there where the action was, is where I began to understand the deeper vision of Ian Berry's photography.

Whilst the *Bang-Bang Club* toured the sites of this internecine conflict, they produced photographs that were spectacular and superficial. Their immediacy told only a fraction of the story.

But what really interested Ian was not so much violence, although he has photographed his fair share of that, but the deeper political stories: those telling of a wide range of conflicts between the black and the white, between the black and the coloured, between the black and the Indian, between the English-speaking and the Afrikaans-speaking whites and between the black and the black.

Ian's images dug deeper to look at the minutiae of life in South Africa at that moment in time. Though more intimate, Ian provided a wider and a more balanced view. The focus of these "conflict" photojournalists was upon those who were fighting for power. This was, without doubt, a very important aspect of the struggle but it failed to show the reality for the majority of the people. As happens in so many of these situations, the majority of citizens wait out the street battles behind closed doors hoping for a better future when it all ends.

The birth pangs of the Rainbow Nation would turn the world of many South Africans upside down, leaving some powerless and shoved to the margins of society. To understand how the seismic shifts in South Africa's social and economic life might be played out, Ian assumed his habitual role of silent hunter, the ghost with the clicking Leica.

With this new understanding of the why and wherefore of Ian's photographs I revisited the images I had been able to source. The process of reacquainting myself with the shapes and shadows in those early monochrome images, and the later colour ones, became a personal journey.

Originally, I had trouble trying to understand how Henri Cartier-Bresson arrived at his *Decisive Moment* but in studying contact sheets and knowing the background behind the photographs, it became clear as to how a story can unfold as you look into the frame, how you can become immersed in an image, or a sequence. You can witness the meaning that lies behind the superficial. I believe it was George Orwell who said, referring to writing, that good writing was like a window of clear glass: you looked through it without distortion or confusion and saw clearly what was on the other side. The same is true of good photography.

Now, Ian will say that he produces his fair share of *ordinary* images, even some which are less than ordinary. I try to tell him that this is his oh-too-critical judgement. From my point of view this is a fair comment. But he remains his sternest critic. Cartier-Bresson told Ian he believed that he was fortunate if he succeeded in shooting one decent shot (one he was happy with) each year.

"As a young photographer, I thought I could take a good photograph each day. Years later I realise the truth of Henri's words." Ian Berry

Philip Jones Griffiths, along with other Magnum photographers who share the photojournalists' background, was correct when he said that we are now in an age of "vision" photography. With digital photography comes the ability to alter and manipulate. The ubiquity of Photoshop and Lightroom, and all the rest of the filters and apps, makes it possible for anyone and their aunty to achieve what were once professional results.

Add to this the gadgets, the gizmos and the range of printers available to one and all these days, and you can become a "professional" in your own front room. With all the exposure in the camera press et cetera we are unable to avoid the various ways of altering an image, for better or for worse. There are tricks and shortcuts, ways of sharpening an image and removing shake and whatever else ails the image. It is all there in the YouTube demonstrations and in the pages of the various photo magazines. Photography has never been so democratic.

The trouble with this is that the "vision" you quest for as you click onto another filter or add a touch of mist is recognising its limitations. This is artistic photography. We must recognise it's not truth.

Appendix IV

The Magic Finger

When all is said and done, it comes down to the response of the photographer to any given situation and then the reaction of the person who looks at the resulting photograph. Making a photograph is about choice: what and when to take the photograph; how to set the camera's various elements; what you include and what you leave out. All this depends upon the cameraman. It is left to their innate "knowing" that will guide their shutter finger.

When we look at a photograph we are seeing a single person's interpretation of what they see. The result will be shaped by how the photographer sees the world, what experience has led him to select that moment and that aspect of any given situation. Should you be like Ian and his peers, who photograph what they see in an honest way, the viewer is left with space to make up their own mind. This becomes a guiding imperative. Let the situation speak for itself and refraining from imposing your views upon the action you are recording.

Amongst the collection of images it is the intensely personal ones that become the most memorable, such as the one we started with: those men in Maseru waiting in the dust storm back in 1960 is so magnificent and multi-layered in its implications.

There are many other Ian Berry images that you could find equally satisfying: the young Buddhist priest with his saffron Superman-cloak and a face full of concentrated joy; the young Chinese woman wearing the latest fashionable dress whilst ignoring and being ignored by the old man with his ghetto-blaster; the various citizens Ian photographed whilst in Odessa and other cities including the incident in Iran when Ian said he: *"knew that one of the women in that bus queue would turn around. There is always one. So, I just waited".*

Sometimes, when Ian is on an assignment that demands images that tell the story there are stand-out pictures that offer the deeper truth: one that I know will stand out is that of the young, fashionable girl in 1968 Prague holding the *Neutrality* placard. There are other Prague images that transcend the mere journalistic. The confrontational images that Ian produced (often the ones that have what Ian calls "shape") have a deeper vision. They transcend the event and speak of a wider humanity. It is Ian's photographic sensibility that we react to instinctively and by so doing we allow these images to "talk" to us.

Ian is reticent about discussing his dangerous assignments. Talking to a couple of his fellow Magnum members, they also find it hard to talk about them. Magnum photographers don't appear to be a boastful lot, nor do they seem to be adrenalin junkies. Chris Steele-Perkins found that assignments in places like Afghanistan lost their glamour once he became a husband and father. Susan Meiselas offered a similar explanation to that of Chris: when you are young it is a different matter; there is excitement and whatever happens won't happen to you.

Besides, failure is not an option and the money is good. It's a *job* (oh yes?) and they are privileged to be there doing it. Some others feel their standing with fellow photographers is enhanced, but this is not for the likes of Chris, Susan, Stuart Franklin and Ian.

Ian takes a somewhat different view. Yes, back in the day, life was exciting and once you were in the middle of the action it was all too fast and the adrenalin pumped around your system. At the end of it all, when your pictures were processed and out there, in print, you had a sense of achievement. But it was a job and one that demanded all your attention and commitment.

Humour

Looking over my narrative to check for factual inaccuracies Ian believes I have, in some cases, made the text far too serious. His memories are full of humour. Yes, there are many occasions when the gods of laughter tripped him up.

Talking about the dangers in the Congo in 1960 Ian prefers to dwell on President Tshombe inviting him for tea and biscuits. This becomes a recurring theme: smile and talk your way out of a situation and end up having tea and cake with someone very important. It happened when he inadvertently photographed the local KGB headquarters whilst on an assignment. Ian believed it to be something entirely different. The building was so ornate it could have been an opera house.

Once again it ended with tea and cake. The Italian prison service offering Ian hospitality after realising why he was there with his cameras, and he wasn't there to try to rescue the recently incarcerated criminals. On the plus side, the Italians provided excellent coffee.

Throughout his working life Ian keeps finding himself in situations where there is an almost farcical side to the event or, at the very least, an element of dark humour. I'm sneaking the word "dark" in here but Ian would probably feel that was too "dark" a word. His view is that the threads of humour that make up the warp and weft of his life are very "bright".

Appendix V

What follows are notes taken during a telephone conversation with Jurgen Schadeberg regarding his time at *Drum* with Ian Berry.

This was recorded on 24th July 2017. Jurgen died some short time after our conversation

1. The relationship between the owner of *Drum* magazine and the editorial staff was often tense.
2. In his time before he joined *Drum* full time Ian Berry had a studio close to one owned by Schadeberg.
3. The history of *Drum* dated back to 1951, when Bob Crisp started a magazine initially called *African Drum*. Jim Bailey invested £1,000 but within a year the magazine was in trouble. Crisp left *Drum* to Bailey who moved it to Johannesburg and invested more money.
4. Crisp went on to start a newspaper he called *Engoli*, which needed a photographer. That photographer was Ian Berry.

5. *Engoli*'s picture editor was Hank Margolies, a cigar-smoking New York American who arrived complete with green eye shades. It was during his time at *Engoli* that Ian Berry admits to gaining experience in structuring an article.
6. Ian began his connection with *Drum* as a freelance. It was only when Tom Hopkinson arrived that it was clear there was a need for a second photographer. Bailey didn't want another white photographer but both Hopkinson and Schadeberg persuaded him that Ian was essential. Ian wanted to work with Hopkinson and took the opportunity offered to join *Drum*.
7. Ian's casual everyday dress was usually corduroy trousers, a silk scarf tied at the neck and tucked under his shirt. Schadeberg remembers Ian was "very trendy" with his fashionable clothing, his little beard and a sports car.
8. Ian had bought the car when it was red but it faded in the South African climate and he had it re-sprayed a silver/grey.
9. When we talked about the reasons why Ian was employed by Hopkinson, Schadeberg acknowledged that Ian is a very good photographer with a style all his own, one that was well suited to photojournalism and reportage.
10. When talking of the problems of photographing in South Africa Schadeberg told me Ian was very courageous and exhibiting this throughout his career. One example he quoted was when, during the Grosvenor Square riots in London at the US embassy in 1968, both Ian and Schadeberg were covering the same event, Schadeberg remembers being hit several times by the police whilst Ian moved amongst the crowd "like a ballet dancer! He was good at avoiding the cops!" Ian's comment on this is that he had a lot of practice in South Africa.

Appendix VI

The relationship between Ian Berry and his good friend and fellow Magnum photographer, the late Philip Jones Griffiths, was one of mutual respect, trust and affection. In 2007, Brigitte Lardinois edited a book called *Magnum, Magnum.* It was published by Thames and Hudson and contained images from every member of Magnum (past and present) chosen by a fellow Magnum photographer. Ian chose images from Philip Jones Griffiths' work and Philip Jones Griffith chose his favourite images from Ian's portfolio. What you will find below are the words Jones Griffiths wrote to accompany his choices:

"Ian Berry was the first Magnum photographer I ever met. He epitomised everything I thought a great photographer should be: egoless, self-effacing, always present but never seen, gliding like a ghost with a clicking Leica. In those days we clearly saw that the photographer was the second half of the equation: the first half was always the subject. How different things have become today, with reality taking second place to the 'vision' of the photographer!

"Ian has showed us the world through his compassionate eyes. He has been everywhere, has seen it all and has never tried to impose a viewpoint on the rest of us. He has simply shown us the way it is, so that we in turn can delight and learn. He has never set up a picture or asked anyone to pose.

"His pictures are reality, and for me this is the indispensable factor that makes photography the most important medium in the history of mankind.

"The old adage, 'f8 and be there,' is one that has guided Ian. He makes Vasco de Gama look like a recluse. He has covered many of the world's most important events and yet is equally passionate in capturing the ebb and flow of ordinary life.

"With Ian form and content meld in an extraordinarily seductive

way that produces photographs that real people yearn to see.

"No photographer could ask for anything more." Philip Jones Griffiths

With grateful thanks for permission to use the quote: Thames and Hudson, London. *Magnum, Magnum,* Edited by Brigitte Lardinois. 2007.

Bibliography

Part I. Books by Ian.

1. Living Apart. (Phaidon Press 1996)
2. The English. Allen Lane (Penguin 1978)
3. Black and Whites, L'Afrique du Sud de Ian Berry. Camera International (Paris) 1988 (Text by François Mitterand et al)
4. Sold into Slavery. Editions CDP. (Malakoff 2008)
5. This is Whitechapel: a companion to the 1972 exhibition.
6. Water. (Gost books 2023)

Part II. Books linked directly to Magnum Photos which feature work by Ian.

1. Magnum Stories. (Phaidon Press 2004)
2. Magnum Revolution, 65 Years of Fighting for Freedom (Prestel Publishing 2012)
3. Magnum Magnum. (Thames and Hudson 2007)
4. A Year in Photography. (Prestel Publishing 2010)
5. Magnum Atlas. (Prestel Publishing 2017)
6. Reading Magnum. (University of Texas Press 2013)
7. Magnum Contact Sheets. Kriston Lubben. (Thames & Hudson Ltd 2014)

Part III. Non-Magnum books that feature work by Ian

1. Various Photography Year Books covering 1959 to 1964, (Fountain Press)
2. Under the Tropic. Tom Hopkinson (Hutchinson 1984). *There are a selection of Ian's photographs including The face that should shock the world (Daily Mirror); Drum's office boy Sidney Andrews after being beaten up by the South African Police.*
3. World Photography, 25 Contemporary Photographers. Edited by Bryn Campbell. (Hamlyn 1981). *Amongst the 25 photographic greats is a section on Ian.*
4. The Long Walk to Freedom. Nelson Mandela (Little, Brown and Company 1994). *The book uses several of Ian's images.*
5. What makes great photography. Val Williams (Francis Lincoln Limited 2013)

Part IV. Books which give a background to Ian's life and times.

1. Travels with a son. John Gale (Hodder and Stoughton 1972). *This covers much of the 1970 journey as described in the text.*
2. Blame me on History. Bloke Modisane (Penguin Modern Classics 1963). *A vivid description of Township life from a Black perspective.*
3. Sharpeville. Tom Lodge, Oxford University Press 2011
4. Defiant Images. Darren & Newbury. (University of South Africa Press 2009)
5. The Bang-Bang Club... snapshots from a hidden war. Marinovich and Silva (Random House 2000). *Though Ian is not mentioned, the background is vividly brought to in contrast to the one Ian experienced.*
6. A Good Looking Corpse. Mike Nicol (Secker and Warburg 1991)
7. An Ordinary Atrocity. Philip Frankel. (Yale University Press 2001)
8. House of Bondage. Ernest Cole. Printed originally in 1967. Now reprinted by Aperture Press in 2020
9. Ernest Cole, Photographer. Knape & Robertson. (Steidl 2010)

Part V. Other sources.

1. Internet. South African History Online has several articles that cover the various periods when Ian was in South Africa. www.sahistory.or.za/article/drum magazine covers Drum but there is no mention of Ian, nor his role in covering Sharpeville.
2. Ian worked for many magazines and his work can be found in copies. Especially relevant would be the Paris Match articles reporting the Prague Spring of 1968.
3. The extensive archive of Sir Tom Hopkinson (1905-1990) cover the Drum years and more. To be found at Cardiff University.

Spreadsheets showing data:

This spreadsheet shows the changing pattern of assignments and who commissions them. It becomes clear that there have been changes in outlets for photojournalists to submit their work. Magazines have become less important for those who work in the current affairs arena. Should Ian have been a photographer of celebrities this may have been a very different profile.

Year	Newspapers	Magazines	Corporate/Advertising	Others/Personal
1959	0	10	0	0
1960	2	15	0	0
1961	0	31	0	0
1962	2	12	4	6
1963	2	13	2	18
1964	13	12	0	0
1965	24	11	0	2
1966	12	9	1	3
1967	17	3	3	8
1968	17	2	2	14
1969	8	4	0	21
1970	1	1	25	17
1971	1	1	1	22
1972	3	1	6	14
1973	0	0	6	10
1974	0	7	9	13
1975	1	3	8	7
1976	0	4	5	14
1977	2	5	11	8
1978	1	10	5	13
1979	0	11	11	5
1980	2	9	11	10
1981	2	11	13	12
1982	4	13	14	6
1983	0	20	11	9
1984	0	6	4	9
1985	1	4	2	13
1986	1	5	7	16
1987	3	12	16	5
1988	0	4	7	9
1989	4	2	14	9
1990	5	6	9	8
1991	1	5	13	5
1992	0	4	17	10
1993	3	4	11	11
1994	2	6	3	22

Both the spreadsheet above and the chart below combine to give you an idea of the number of assignments Ian has worked on per year. The source for this data is his spend on his domestic, family and holiday photography. It should be noted that this raw data gives no idea of just how long each assignment or commission took.

Year	Number of assignments
1959	10
1960	21
1961	31
1962	24
1963	35
1964	25
1965	34
1966	26
1967	31
1968	35
1969	33
1970	44
1971	25
1972	24
1973	16
1974	29
1975	23
1976	22
1977	26
1978	29
1979	27
1980	32
1981	38
1982	37
1983	40
1984	19
1985	20
1986	29
1987	36
1988	20
1989	29
1990	28
1991	24
1992	31
1993	29
1994	33
1995	35
1996	48
1997	27
1998	31
1999	41
2000	34
2001	26
2002	21
2003	15
2004	14
2005	19
2006	33
2007	18
2008	22
2009	24
2010	16
2011	12
2012	18
2013	25
2014	26
2015	20
2016	20
2017	34
Total	1594
Average number of jobs/year	27